Modern Tennis Doubles

Modern Tennis Doubles

STAN SMITH & BOB LUTZ

with Larry Sheehan

Illustrated by Jim McQueen

ATHENEUM / SMI   NEW YORK   1975

Copyright © 1975 by Stan Smith, Bob Lutz and Larry Sheehan
All rights reserved
Library of Congress catalog card number 75–13514
ISBN 0–689–10687–4
Published simultaneously in Canada by McClelland and Stewart Ltd.
Composition by Dix Typesetting Co., Inc., Syracuse, New York
Printed by Carney Printing Co., Nashville, Tennessee
Bound by Nicholstone Book Bindery, Inc., Nashville, Tennessee
Designed by Kathleen Carey
First Edition

CONTENTS

PART I

Principles

CHAPTER 1

Why Doubles Demands a Special Approach

TENNIS DOUBLES IS NOT simply a crowded version of singles, though that is the way many weekend players go at the game.

This misinterpretation seems to be especially true in America. Our emphasis on the values of rugged individualism is carried to an illogical extreme in the way tennis has been imparted to the mass of new players. We have insisted on teaching our recreational tennis players the strokes, tactics, and mental attitudes needed for the one-on-one game of singles—and then sent them out to play doubles all the time!

Weekend doubles players are further indoctrinated in singles techniques today by the favoritism shown that format of play by tournament directors and tournament coverage by the media. Actually, this is changing slightly as more money pours into doubles events and the fans sense that more of the pros are taking their doubles game seriously.

But basically, singles matches get more of the grandstand-court assignments and most of the TV time. So, in the mind of the typical newcomer to the sport, the only proper way to consummate one's own development as a player is by standing alone and batting aces through some villainous foe. Which is precisely the wrong approach for doubles.

In truth, the singles bias of the tournament people and the networks is justified. Doubles may be quite intriguing to watch if you know what to look for, but it is often less compelling than singles at its best. If you are a stranger to the particular teams, and if the points are run off in machine-gun fashion, doubles play often can seem repetitious and dull. Singles, on the other hand, is interesting to watch even if you don't know much about the players, or the sport for that matter. Like bullfighting or boxing, singles has great potential for drama and emotional involvement. It belongs in the spotlight.

But in this book we want to talk about the game as it is played by the majority of tennis buffs, not as it is watched by spectators. As a participant sport, doubles is the popular format in tennis—even when played incorrectly—simply because it is more sociable and less tiring. It provides the same outlet for friendly competition that the weekend foursome does in golf and, also in a similar fashion to golf, is quite likely the backbone of the game's broad appeal.

Doubles also makes more sense wherever tennis courts are crowded, which seems to be almost everywhere nowadays. And when it comes to renting court time indoors for the off-season, doubles is twice as economical as singles.

For all these reasons we have an increasing number of tennis players today who are exclusively or primarily doubles players, but who, because of improper instruction or through misplaced enthusiasm about the brand of tennis they see on television, are actually playing the game with *singles* techniques.

((4))

HOW DOUBLES DIFFERS FROM SINGLES ON RETURN OF SERVE

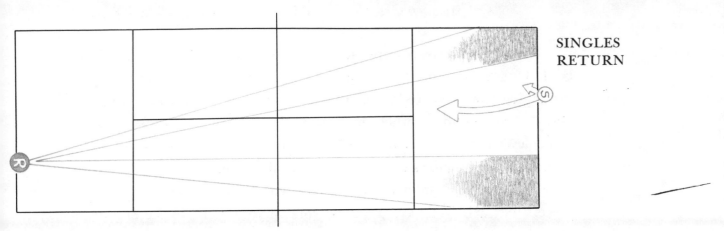

SINGLES
RETURN

The addition of alleys and a second opponent create major tactical and stroking differences between singles and doubles. In a typical return of serve in singles, the receiver can play the width of the court, and, in hitting to the more open corner, begin the process of maneuvering his or her opponent out of position. The singles receiver can clear the net (see below) by three or four feet on the return with relative impunity.

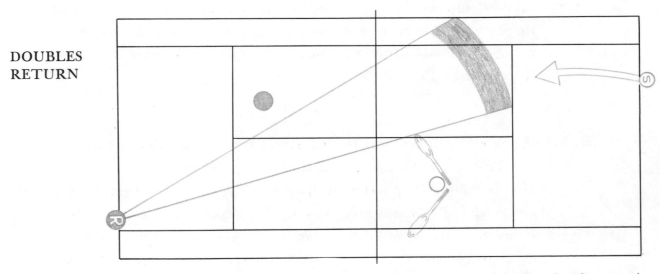

DOUBLES
RETURN

In a typical return of serve in doubles, the receiver's margin for error is greatly reduced. The opposing net player effectively blocks almost half of the opposite side of the court. The server, in moving up to the service line following serve, cramps the receiver's style even more by cutting down on the playable depth of the court on that side. The receiver must attempt to clear the net on the return (see below) by little more than a foot. If the ball is floated back high, either opponent may move in and volley it away. The receiver must play a careful shot and wait for a later opportunity to maneuver the opponents out of position with a low volley or lob, or force an error with a hard ground stroke.

singles return

doubles return

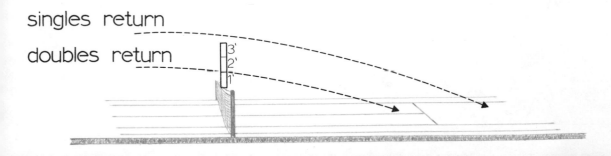

It is to these players in particular that we address ourselves in this book. Our hope is to turn you into more effective doubles players by explaining the major technical, tactical, and psychological differences between singles and doubles, and then showing you the strokes and strategies that have worked well for the Smith-Lutz combination, against the best doubles teams in professional tennis today.

We believe this information not only will make you better doubles players but, once you have put it to work in your game to the best of your ability, also will make your doubles matches a lot more *interesting*.

Our approach to the doubles game combines purposeful attack, sound defense, and smooth teamwork in a way that actually increases the variety of strokes that you produce and the shot situations that you face during play. In time, you will develop more consistent, well-rounded shot-making skills that should also come in handy in your singles play. But most of all, you will get more fun and excitement out of your doubles. And that, we firmly believe, is the most important ingredient of all.

We think there are three big differences between doubles and singles.

First, there are different values to be placed on the tennis strokes used in doubles, and technical differences in how some of the strokes are produced. For example, you need a dependably accurate serve rather than the powerful flat serve that a good singles player tries to develop. You need to be able to *return* serve with greater consistency in doubles, whereas in singles you can go for broke on returns. In doubles you must have a good volley stroke, because there is no way you can avoid being at the net some of the time. In singles you can get away with mediocre volleying, if your backcourt game is solid, and perhaps still make it to the final of your club championship.

((6))

Second, there are major *tactical* differences of position and shot-selection in doubles, occasioned by the change in court dimension and number of players. The doubles court is seven hundred square feet larger in area than the singles court, due to the addition of the two four-and-a-half-foot-wide lanes, or alleys, running the sides of the court. Superficially there is more lateral area to hit into, encouraging wider shots rather than the deep shots that are so valuable in singles. But the presence of a second player on the other side of the net actually gives you less open space to aim for than you would have in singles, so accuracy in picking your angles is a must.

Your shots need not be spectacular in doubles, as they often have to be in singles to win a point against a player of equal ability, but they must be exceedingly well placed. Thus errors of racket technique will be severely punished. You can get away with a fair number of mis-hits in singles if you have other things going for you, but if you hit a high ball in doubles, or a haphazard off-the-wood shot, there is always a player hovering near on the other side, ready to crack the high ball away for a winner—more often than not, right through your hapless partner.

Conversely, since you yourself have a partner, there is less open space for you to defend on your side of the net. Though the total doubles court area is greater, you have only about two-thirds as much territory to protect as you would on a singles court. You may have to stretch for more shots—worthy opponents will see to that—but you won't have to outright *run* for nearly so many as you would in a tough game of singles.

Finally, there are significant psychological and emotional differences in the game of doubles. If singles is akin to chess in the sort of single-mindedness, will, and agony-of-ego factors riding on each encounter, then doubles is more like bridge: How well you play your cards depends in large part on how well your partner plays his. And the interaction among four different personalities on the court, within teams and between teams, is worthy of endless fascinating analysis.

In comparing singles and doubles, people sometimes mistakenly think of the latter as a more genteel version of the game. Singles-only snobs, if they happen to be men, speak of doubles as a game "for ladies," and if they happen to be women, call it an amusement "for old men."

Such critics are blaming the game instead of the lackadaisical performance of the players, which is where the blame really belongs. They are making fun of a kind of "Sunday doubles" that may well have been widely practiced, to a certain extent even among the top players, in an earlier era. Sunday doubles amounted to polite exchanges between teams of confirmed baseliners, with an absence of poaches and overheads and a minimum of volleys. Maybe it still exists in patches today, but it is no longer prevalent even among people who don't quite know how to play doubles, but who are full of passion for smacking the ball and politeness be damned. In short, today's doubles game offers as much potential for speed, power, and subtlety as the most aggressive singles nut could wish.

Another false impression some players have formed about doubles is that it corrupts their singles game. As we mentioned earlier, doubles can actually *improve* your singles game by broadening your shot-making range. True, there are players at any level, including some of the pros, who are absolute loners and mavericks in their tennis for one reason or another, and they are incapable of playing good doubles. But they are a minority. As a general rule, the two forms of tennis are mutually enriching—provided the player knows how to adapt his strokes and strategies in going from one to the other.

Maybe the best answer to the question of compatibility between singles and doubles is the phenomenal record of the major modern

HOW DOUBLES DIFFERS FROM SINGLES IN ACTION

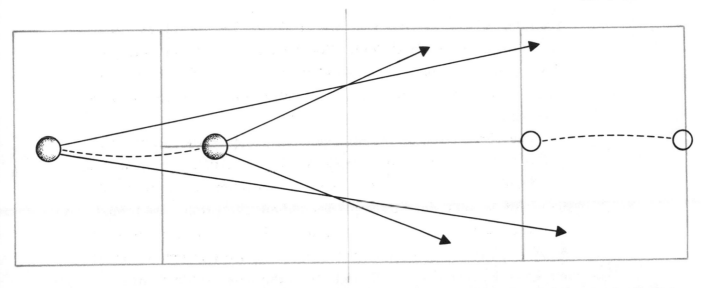

Although the court is narrower by nine feet for singles than it is for doubles, the tendency in singles is to bring the action to the sides. Ground strokes that are deep and steady are a big asset in singles. So is the endurance required to produce the sequence of them that will finally yield a chance to come in to net, or an opening for a put-away.

DOUBLES PLAY

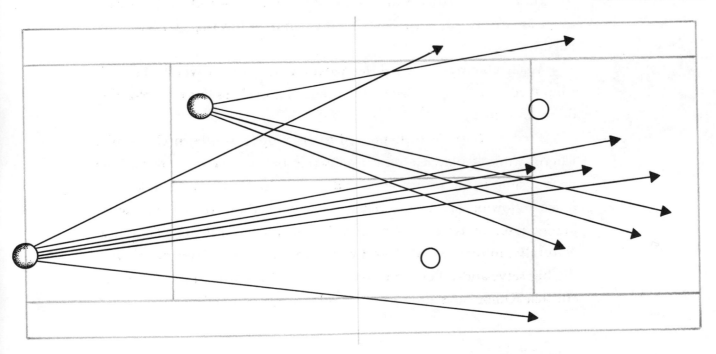

In good doubles action, more balls are hit down the middle than down the sides. The presence of two opponents, each guarding a lane, makes the down-the-line passing shot a riskier proposition than it is in singles. Hitting down the middle assures keeping the ball in play and also presents a possibly confusing choice to the opponents as to who will play the ball. Since doubles players move to net more quickly, there are fewer ground strokes exchanged. Short hard or angled volleys or smashes win points outright in doubles; good ground strokes sometimes set up winners or force errors by the opponents.

Australian players over the years in both forms. Lew Hoad, Ken Rose-wall, Roy Emerson, Fred Stolle, Rod Laver, Tony Roche, and John Newcombe—all of these champions have been able to shift gears effort-lessly in going from one format to another, sometimes in the same afternoon.

It is also interesting to note that one could pick the doubles pair-ings out of a hat from among these Aussies and still come up with a formidable combination. This confirms two other points about the nature of doubles. First, these players without exception were brought up in tennis as *attackers*. Their developed instinct to come to net at every opportunity, combined with their uniformly strong volleying, made them experts at doubles right from the start. Another advantage of the group as a whole, as far as doubles play is concerned, has been their loyalty to each other as friends who have trained and traveled together for years and who have joined forces for Australia in such inter-nation events as Davis Cup and World Cup. They have built up the kind of familiarity with each other as players—and faith in each other as persons—that can pay big dividends in forming doubles part-nerships.

What about our own development as doubles players? Maybe it would be revealing to briefly trace how we evolved into an effective doubles team . . .

First of all, we both happened to grow up in southern California, where tennis is played almost exclusively on fast cement courts. The native game is the power serve and, more important for doubles, the quick following of serve to net to pounce on the return. The native heroes in tennis as we grew up were Jack Kramer and Pancho Gonzalez. Naturally, in our awe of these living legends, we associated them with the big serve-and-volley game as used in singles. (Much later we found out that Kramer was also one of the all-time great doubles players.) But as we grew up we also became conscious of the challenge and the chance for a bit of glory in doubles, too. That was mainly because we observed the great success enjoyed by Dennis Ralston and Rafael Osuna as doubles partners for the University of Southern California tennis team. We would watch them play their home matches for USC and attend many of their practice sessions at the L.A. Tennis Club. We were especially impressed when, in 1960, they became the youngest doubles champions in the history of Wimbledon.

Meanwhile, we were developing our tennis games along separate paths that would eventually converge at USC. Bob began taking lessons at age nine from Ray Casey, a big left-handed pro in Santa Monica. Casey happened to like doubles and in the course of the next few years played a lot of it with Lutz. As a leftie who always took the second court in competitive doubles, Casey tended to groom Bob's doubles stroke-making for that side and, in fact, Lutz became a natural backhand court player. In singles Casey encouraged Lutz to rush net following serve, even though this tactic spelled certain and consistent defeat for Bob for several years, as opponents in his age group simply lobbed over his head from the baseline. But as Lutz grew taller and his volleying grew sharper, he became more difficult to pass. Casey's teaching began to pay off and Bob started putting away his old rivals—the ones who had beaten him from the baseline—with great ease.

Smith didn't take up tennis seriously until much later than Lutz, when he was fifteen. At this age he was already big enough to play and profit through serve-and-volley tennis, which he began to develop under Pancho Segura in a stimulating clinic that great strategist ran for kids in Pasadena. As a six-footer Stan had the reach at net, backed up by his overall athletic ability and his quickly developing overhead stroke, to be a highly desirable doubles partner . . .

It was only a matter of time before we would meet, and click. We got to know each other and to play doubles together regularly when we decided to try to follow in the footsteps of Ralston and Osuna and enrolled at USC. Coach George Toley further groomed our doubles skills, particularly in volleying and in match strategy, in leading us to the National Intercollegiate Championship in doubles in both 1967 and 1968. (We also won the singles title for USC in those years, Lutz in 1967, Smith in 1968.)

Playing on a team increased our respect for doubles for the simple reason that our matches with teams from other schools were contested on the basis of points won in six singles matches and three doubles matches. Points won from the doubles could easily determine the outcome of the overall match, so we practiced and played doubles earnestly. (Most better players who get the chance to compete for high school or college teams learn the value of doubles and the basic approach to playing it, but in their early adult life tend to concentrate on singles. Ironically, the mass of weekend players who end up playing doubles most of the time have had no background at all in that form of competition.)

In the same period we won the hard-court doubles and the clay-court doubles, but our first efforts out on the men's circuit got nowhere either in singles or doubles. In a way this further strengthened our doubles partnership simply because, upon getting knocked out of the men's tournaments in the early rounds, we had nothing better to do but spend the rest of the week practicing with each other. In time, we did break through, with our major wins of that early period being the 1968 doubles at Forest Hills, the 1970 doubles in the Australian Open, and various wins for the United States in its successful defense of Davis Cup from 1968 to 1970.

We separated for a couple of years when Lutz turned professional for World Championship Tennis and Smith joined the Army, the latter continuing his winning Davis Cup play, with Erik van Dillen as doubles

DOUBLES ANGLES

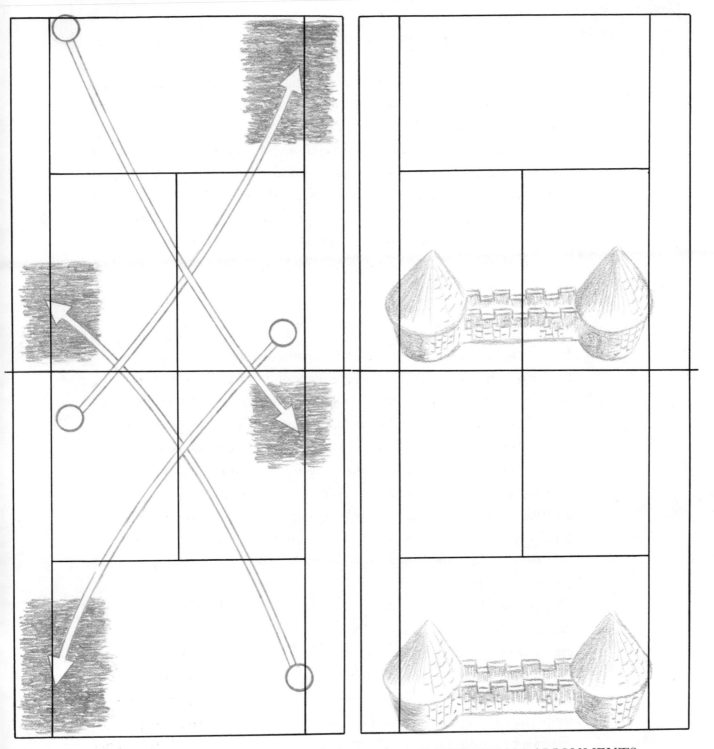

VULNERABLE TEAM ALIGNMENTS   SOUND TEAM ALIGNMENTS

In singles, players may remain at the base line following serve or return without jeopardy except against a consistent attacker, and wait for the chance to come to net. In doubles, players must strive to come to net immediately following serve or return, simply because the usual team configurations at the outset of a point are highly vulnerable to angled shots.

Doubles partners must establish themselves side by side at net in an offensive position—or, if necessary, at the base line in a defensive position—in order to protect against angled shots into the gaping holes between partners, at the start of each point.

partner. In the meantime our singles games developed apace. Smith won Forest Hills in 1971 and Wimbledon in 1972, the two great titles, and Lutz won the United States Professional Championship at Longwood in 1972 before a knee operation disabled him temporarily. In any case, the victories earned us a respect as individual singles players that could not help strengthening our image as a doubles combination, as far as our opponents were concerned. Shortly after we were reunited as a team, we won the first World Championship Tennis doubles final in 1972 in Montreal, splitting $40,000—the biggest first prize for doubles in the history of tennis.

In a sense, the Montreal doubles tournament marked a turning point for tennis doubles generally, and the increase in prize money for doubles that has occurred since then has considerably upgraded the doubles game among both pros and fans. WCT has continued to invest heavily in doubles in the belief there is a growing public interest in doubles battles between committed teams. The major national championships, including Forest Hills and Wimbledon, have jacked up their doubles awards. And for 1975, Commercial Union, sponsor of the nine-month-long Grand Prix circuit, instituted a doubles "bonus pool" for the first time, designating some $100,000 to be awarded to the top doubles teams of the year.

We used to feel that Smith and Lutz were about the only men's doubles team, outside of the various Australian duos, with any concrete tradition of playing together, and of really having developed a sense of playing doubles as a team. Now, with all the money invested in doubles by sponsors, a large number of younger players are taking the doubles game seriously. They are spending more time in practice sessions as doubles teams, talking about doubles more, analyzing other teams in action, and playing their doubles matches with a lot more effort and intensity.

Even mixed doubles, which relatively few pros of either sex have taken seriously, is being played more earnestly in some tournaments where the money is right. The men are overcoming their hangups about banging balls at women playing net, and the women—to the astonishment of some of the men—are banging them right back. Money has brought out the killer instinct in both sexes, apparently, and in any case has definitely added spice to what has been until now a bland and perfunctory event.

So the future looks bright for doubles at the pro level. Now, let's see what we can do to make doubles better and brighter for you . . .

CHAPTER 2

Principles of Modern Doubles Play

THE DOUBLES SENSE is a knack that has to be acquired.

Learning to play with the doubles sense—with the instincts and reactions that will cause you to execute the right shots in the right situations—comes out of the experience of consciously applying basic doubles principles to your moves and actions.

We think there are four interrelated principles underlying all good doubles play. They affect your stroke-making, your positioning on the court, your relation to your partner, and your control over your opponents through match strategy.

These principles must be well understood, and at first consciously applied, to make sure the desirable actions occur out on the court. After a while, much less conscious effort will be needed to get the kind of results you want.

Let's examine the four principles in detail and see how they fit into actual doubles play.

PLAY THE BALL

Playing the ball means not letting the ball play you—in other words, taking the initiative and moving forward to meet the ball on as many shots as you can. Hitting off your back foot encourages defensive stroke-making and shots that give the opponents a moment's extra time to steal a march on you. Hitting off your front foot, while the ball is still on the rise, builds firmer shots with lower trajectories and more top-spin. It also gets the ball back over the net with less time elapsed, forcing the opponents to react sooner and without as much preparation.

In doubles you do not have the luxury of pauses for reflection or leisurely stroking—as you might have against good but passive singles opponents—because you have twice as much opposition to contend with. Both time and space are more compressed, and if you do not act quickly and decisively, one of your opponents will surely pounce on your shot. That is why a good retrieving team won't win in doubles nearly so often as a good attacking team. Good doubles teams are almost constantly in motion—no one is a statue.

Quickness definitely counts for more in doubles than in singles. If you are quick off the mark following your serve, you will be in a position to take the return from a firm volleying stance well into the court. If you receive serve with the proper alertness, you will actually move *diagonally* in the court to meet the oncoming ball, rather than directly to the side in anticipation of where it will bounce up. That will permit you to meet the ball earlier, and at the same time avoid being pulled wide and vulnerable. You will also add one more option to your possible returns, since it is always easier to hit down the line on a return when you are going toward the ball and not standing still or falling back from it.

Good poaching is the most dramatic example of playing the ball. By moving quickly and intercepting an opponent's shot, you seize the play in an authoritative manner against which there is seldom any riposte. Moving toward the ball gives your volley stroke firmness and direction. Otherwise, you are not volleying the ball so much as rebounding it.

In doubles you are responsible not just for getting the ball back, but also for how your opponent is able to return *your* shot. If you do not keep him on the defensive, your team will pay the penalty. That is why you can't make shots at the ball's convenience. The more difficulties you create for your opponents, the more weak returns they will set up for you and your partner to exploit.

It is not enough simply to try to stroke aggressively on every shot.

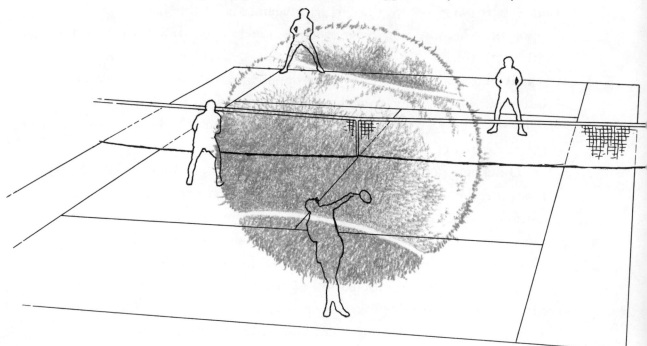

DOUBLES PRINCIPLE 1   PLAY THE BALL—DON'T LET THE BALL PLAY YOU

With the extra personnel on hand for doubles—one extra on your side of the net and one extra on the other side—and with the subtler tactical requirements of the game, players more readily forget that the ball remains the most important object involved in the action. Remaining fully aware of the ball helps keep your eye on it better and encourages you to move into shots more aggressively. It also sets you thinking in terms of moving the ball into a position that is untenable for the opponents, or at least will force them onto the defensive.

You also must *place* your shots aggressively. Calculating where you are going to put the ball on the opposite side is also part of playing the ball. In serving, it means consciously directing the ball to the receiver's weak side. In returning, it means placing the ball out of reach of the net man and at the feet of the server. In volleying close in, it means punching the ball back either at an angle or right through the opposing net man. So aim everything you hit—it will sharpen all your strokes.

Maybe it should be obvious that playing the ball implies keeping your eye on the ball in the first place, but it's wise for doubles players to remind themselves of this basic from time to time—especially if they're mis-hitting certain shots and can't figure out why. In doubles there are more distractions than in singles, and it is simply much easier to take your eye off the ball. Sudden moves by your opponents or your own partner can draw your attention. So can too much worry about where you want to put the ball in the first place, or your desire to quickly follow your shot into a better position on the court.

So hit the ball first on serve, return, volley, and overhead—then follow through.

CONTROL THE NET

In singles, when you come to net, the chief danger you face is the passing shot. When you come to net in doubles, the passing shot is not much of a threat, simply because the opponent has much less space to pass you in. So you really have no excuse to hang back. In singles, it is possible—and quite common, except among the top men pros and a few of the women pros—to play a winning brand of tennis from the baseline. If you have the ground strokes, the endurance, and the patience, you can do it. But in doubles you *must* control the net.

DOUBLES PRINCIPLE 2   CONTROL THE NET

In singles, solid ground strokes from the base line form the basis for your control of your opponent's moves and the course of the match. In doubles, control comes only when you and your partner are in a position to hit down on the opponents, and that means moving into a close position at net.

It is hard to win a point from the baseline in doubles mainly because of the presence of the opposing net man, who can effectively defend against shots hit to one half of the court, and threaten shots hit to the other half. It is possible to lob him or hit through him from the baseline, but then you are depending on an exceptionally good shot by you, or an error by him, to prolong the point if not to win it, and in the long run you would not score as much off him as he would off you.

Playing from the backcourt, you will have to hit a fairly good shot every time against a good team, or you'll be in trouble. But when you move into net, you sometimes have to do no more than simply get the ball back in order to win points. That's because you are so close that the opponents often won't have time to run down your shot or prepare adequately on shots hit at them.

The best way to undo the opposing net man's advantageous position is to come to net and hit shots that destroy him or, thanks to the angle, can afford to ignore him—in other words, to take control of the net from him. Whichever team controls the net wins the point, in 90 percent of the cases.

Control of the net does not simply mean being up at net. It means being in a ready position at the net—both you and your partner—and also being in possession of an effective volley stroke and, for use against the lob, an effective overhead.

If your volley and overhead strokes are weak, you should still try to come to net as frequently as you can following your serve or a good return of serve. Why? It's the only way to build up experience of these strokes under combat conditions. And, even if you are a paper tiger at net while still learning your volley, your presence may intimidate opponents a bit and perhaps force an error.

Until you learn to back up your serve by moving in and making a good first volley, you will not hold any particular advantage in serving —your opponents will be able to take the offensive with a good return.

The idea of moving to net actually reinforces the principle of playing the ball—moving in as much as possible to meet every shot— and it also helps build sound stroke-making. If you are thinking of going to net following your serve, you will be more likely to swing *through* the ball properly—and not hit *at* the ball as so often happens among beginning and intermediate players—as you bring your back foot around and into the court. On your returns, you will be more likely to put your weight into each shot if you are predisposed to move forward after completing the stroke.

One is obviously handicapped in trying to apply the principle of moving to net in actual play if there is fear of being near the net. Such fear not only often keeps many players from moving into good offensive positions on the court in doubles, but renders them useless if and when they do get there. Your best shield from anxieties about being hit by the ball is a good solid volley stroke. But you can also easily prove to yourself that the ball isn't likely to hurt you, even if it does hit you— at least not at the speeds it travels at the club level of play. During practice sometime, try catching hard-hit balls at net with your bare hand. If you can catch the ball, it also means you can get out of its way in time to avoid being hit—and, more important, that you can volley it.

It takes some time and patience, and a bit of adventurousness, to play at net in the early stages of one's development in tennis. But once you are comfortable there psychologically, and are confident in your volley, you will begin to relish playing forward, because that's where most of the points are decided, and the action there has a spontaneity and quickness that can be exhilarating.

There are several specific advantages to being at net. The net itself is no longer a significant hurdle for you to consider in sending the ball back. You are able to see the opponents and their side of the court better. You are in a position to exploit a greater percentage of area on the other side, and at a wider choice of angles. Finally, when at net you can meet the ball sooner after an opponent has hit it, and so return it before he is fully prepared to do anything about it.

Naturally, your better opponents will be trying to get control of the net in the same way and often at the same times. From some preliminary swordplay from opposing baselines, good doubles teams plunge into skirmishes at net, with their volley strokes being the equivalent of daggers. In such in-fighting it is usually the quickness of reflexes and the sharpness of the volleying that determines who finally wins the point.

WORK AS A TEAM

Later we'll devote a chapter to various specific ways in which you and your doubles partner can improve communication and performance as a team. For now, bear in mind that when playing doubles you are a twosome on the court, playing against another twosome, and above all, not against each other. One plus one equals less than two in a poor doubles combination. But a really effective combination is actually *more* than the sum of its parts.

In doubles you must think, feel, act, and react as a team. The two areas in which teamwork shows up dramatically are your movements in the court and the shots you select to make.

Good partners play the court as a team, moving together up to net and back again as necessary, and shifting from side to side whenever wide shots take one player somewhat off the court, so that the other partner, in moving a step or two, keeps the line of attack intact.

For two players to work together well as a team in covering the court, each player must continually shift or adjust position, following every shot by his or her side, in order to be in the best possible spot for handling the range of likely returns by the opponent. The server must serve, and then move into the court to the center of possible returns by the receiver. The receiver must return, and then hop back into the middle of the returner's half of the court. The net player must volley, and then step forward or to the side with racket high and ready to volley again. The player who lobs must move to the spot from which fielding the inevitable overhead will be easiest.

Recovering your proper court position following each shot in this manner is a fundamental in singles as well as doubles. The difference

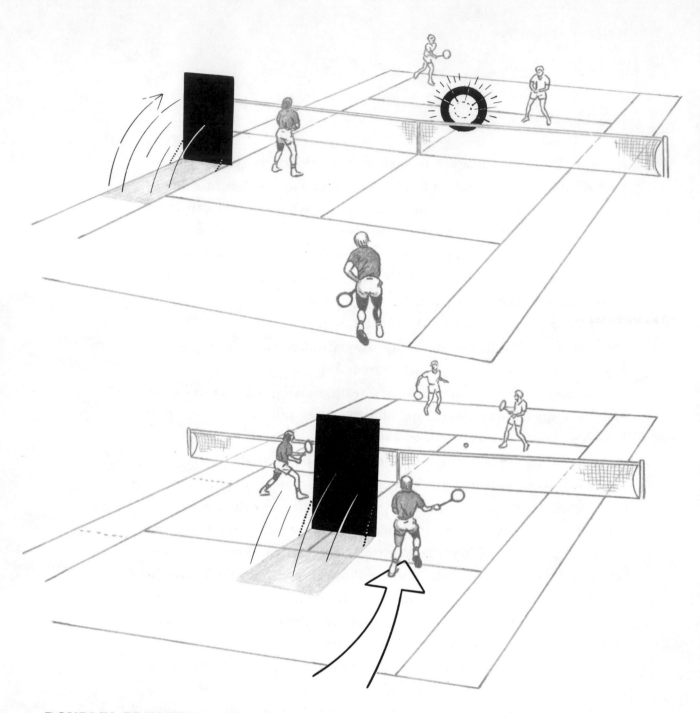

DOUBLES PRINCIPLE 3   WORK AS A TEAM

In doubles, one plus one will equal more than the sum of its parts if both players hit shots as a team and move as a team. For example, by consciously serving to your opponent's weaker or backhand side, you greatly reduce the chance of your partner being attacked on the return. And when you move to net following the serve, you create a line of attack with your partner that further inhibits the receiver.

in doubles is that you must always recover in relation to your partner's shots, as well as to your own.

If a player does not come in following his serve, his partner is effectively stranded up at net. He has to keep looking back to see what's going on. The opponents have a big gap to exploit with a variety of angled shots.

If a player does not retreat, following a good lob by the opponents, the same vulnerable one-up, one-back situation develops.

How do you make shots "as a team"? There are numerous ways in which good doubles players produce their strokes in consideration of their partners.

For instance, when you serve to an opponent's backhand, or weaker side, you are, in effect, serving "as a team," because you are reducing the chances of your partner at net getting drilled by a strong forehand return. When you get your first serve in consistently, you are greatly increasing your partner's margin of safety at net—and also increasing his potential value to the team. He has more chances to cross and poach on weak returns, and so to help get you through your service game with less pressure.

A big test of teamwork comes on shots hit down the middle, or lobs that apparently could be fielded by either partner. In such situations one player almost always has a slight but real edge over the other in his ability to handle the shot at hand. You may be inches closer, or the ball may be coming to your stronger volleying side, or you may have the quickness or the momentum to get a jump on the lob. Good teams with the experience of having played matches together before instinctively know which player will take the ball. Poor or less experienced doubles partners will either both withdraw, leaving no one to try to prolong the point, or both go after the ball, leaving openings to one or both sides that the opponents will be able to take advantage of if the ball is retrieved.

The moves and shots you make on a doubles court largely reflect your strategic approach to the match, but it should also be noted under "teamwork" that both partners must agree on the best means of attack and defense, in consideration of their own strengths and weaknesses and those of their opponents. For example, should one of you decide to consistently attack the serve of one of the opponents, while the other proceeds on the assumption that trying to break the *other* opponent's serve is the better course of action, then you may cancel out each other's efforts.

MAKE IT HAPPEN

You can't wait for something good to happen in singles any more than in doubles, but a passive, unplanned approach is more quickly a disaster in doubles because thoughtlessly placed serves, returns, and volleys can be immediately attacked. In doubles you must constantly create your own opportunities through a strategic approach that is jointly conceived, organized, and executed.

In our own experience on the circuit we have sometimes gone into a match with "singles confidence"—as individuals we perhaps had a record of victories against the individuals comprising the other team— only to find ourselves a set and a half down before we knew it. We soon discovered that you can never win in doubles on the strength of your singles reputation, or with any kind of a casual or smug attitude. From the start, you must feel you are taking a certain number of calculated risks in trying to force mistakes by the opponents, break their service, and gain the momentum.

In singles you tend to go for winners sooner, but in doubles you

DOUBLES PRINCIPLE 4   MAKE IT HAPPEN

If singles is a battle of wills, then doubles may be described as a battle of wits. Without a logical game plan, based on your team's strengths and the opposing team's weaknesses, even highly talented tennis players will not succeed in doubles. And this game plan must be consciously and constantly attended to. "Computerize" the information in your mind so that it contains your main plan as well as a number of variations, plus an alternate plan if things don't go well. And before every point push a button on your "computer" to confirm or revise your strategy.

must play to safe spots on the court until you get the opportunity for a winning shot. Only then can you take a chance and try to put it away and win the point.

There is room for more forethought in doubles than there is in singles. If you are serving or receiving, you are trying to establish a pattern of play that, after a couple of exchanges, will give you the chance to go for the winner. If you are playing net, you are trying to support or disrupt whichever pattern is beginning to emerge.

Even the low-percentage shot is premeditated in good doubles. You go for the winner at what seems like an inopportune time, not simply to "keep the other guy honest"—by forcing him to remain alert over a broader spectrum of play—but to try to keep your opponent from perceiving your basic strategy and thus your main pattern of play.

Momentum seems to be able to shift even more easily in doubles than it can in singles. If you have the momentum, you must concentrate on the first few points of your own serve. You want to play loose but not lax—you can't go unconscious—in order to continue to draw off the energies that have been serving you so well so far. If you don't have the momentum, you must tighten up your play—without tightening your muscles—and focus on breaking the opponent's serve, which requires taking more chances, not by making silly mistakes but by mixing up your returns more.

Between teams of fairly equal ability and experience, momentum may not come into play for many of those games during which both sides hold serve. You must then patiently adhere to your basic strategy —or change to your alternate strategy if the basic strategy is failing— until the ad point comes up that swings things around to your side. But breaking serve does not give you the momentum for keeps. In fact, it sometimes inspires the other team so much that they immediately break back and gain the momentum on you.

If you were to diagram a closely contested doubles match in these terms, you might draw a long, gradually ascending line to indicate the uphill battle to get hold of the momentum, then a level line to indicate a plateau of sorts when the momentum is not firmly on either side, and finally an abruptly descending line to show the swift end of the match which comes once the momentum shifts decisively. It is that relatively short time in the plateau area when the issue of who gets the winning momentum seems to be fully resolved. It may correspond to a sequence of only a few games—which may come anywhere in the match—during which both doubles teams are clearly fighting for mastery. This is the time when it is critical to continue your planned attack, neither switching without good reason to another strategy, nor withdrawing in your aggressiveness in the hope that your opponents will make the errors that will help you win.

Appearances can be deceiving. One team may be winning serve easily, while the other must struggle each game, and thus seemingly have the momentum. But this could shift suddenly if, for example, that second team happens to break serve on a couple of fluke points.

Or take two teams who have played each other frequently, with one side winning the vast majority of matches. On the surface it may appear that the teams are evenly matched. But if one has a history of dominance, that team will possess a big psychological edge, and it will be very hard for the other team to acquire the momentum. One lucky shot by the historically superior team may confirm the inferior team's low opinion of its chances and effectively end the match right there. Only a solid positive attitude can prevent this from happening.

Good doubles teams learn to *start fast*—with super concentration— and *never play casually*. Other than that advice, there really is no single tip for getting the momentum, or for keeping it after you've got it, or for getting it back after you've lost it. But you should always be aware of its existence in every match and be aware also that it will settle on your side of the net only if you *make it happen*. It's a kind of wind that fills your team's sails and brings you to victory. That is what you are fighting for from the start, first with a shot, then with a point, then with a game, then with a set, and finally with the match. And sometimes it is not until the last point of the match that you can safely say that the mysterious ingredient called momentum is truly on your side.

CHAPTER 3

The Shifting Doubles Roles and How to Play Them

Now let's look at how the principles of modern doubles affect your varying responsibilities in the course of a match.

Playing doubles may be compared to a drama in which you rotate among four distinctly different roles. These are the roles of server, server's partner, receiver, and receiver's partner. Good doubles players learn each role by heart—they know the special chores and worries they have in each slot—and move effortlessly among all four roles in a match. Each role comes with its own unique responsibilities . . . and potential for dramatic action.

In these characterizations, we'll confine ourselves to the moderately aggressive brand of doubles that is exemplified by the best doubles teams today, in the belief that such doubles, in whole or in part, is within reach of the majority of doubles players at the club level, too. Thus we are predicating our recommendations for each of the roles on the assumption that, in most cases, both teams will be attempting to gain control of net following serves. Later we'll deal with the special approaches dictated by servers who hang back at the baseline, by receivers who depend on the lob as their main weapon of return, and by other inherently vulnerable doubles tactics. We'll also suggest ways in which to deal with the unusual obstacles posed by left-handers, topspin fanatics, and other off-the-beaten-track doubles opponents. At this point, our main wish is to impart to you an overall sense of the principal roles and responsibilities in playing maximum-effort doubles.

We should also mention, for the record, that our doubles philosophy applies equally to men's doubles, women's doubles, and mixed doubles, so we will seldom if ever make asides on behalf of one type only. It is true that we are usually advocating such aggressive tactics as moving in following serve and return, poaching, and occasional targeting on players at net on returns, volleys, and overheads. Do these tactics really apply to all of doubles? In mixed doubles, for instance, men's firing cannonballs at women players positioned at net has been generally frowned upon.

Actually, we believe such problems must be resolved according to the level of play, not the type of play. There really is no good reason not to hit at a woman player in a serious match between more advanced teams of fairly equal abilities and experience. On the other hand, however, it would be blatantly poor sportsmanship for a superior player to hit hard balls directly at a net player, whether male or female, who is still relatively unschooled in the game, because the chances are that the superior player could win the point in one of several different ways. But if the woman is the equal of the man, targeting on her may be justified at times—and many women today would not have it otherwise. (Incidentally, your best possible target area, when hitting at an opponent, is the player's armpit on the side he or she holds the racket. That jams the player's response but good.)

Obviously, discretion, common sense, and a sense of fair play must be invoked at times in doubles as in any sport. Our wish is not to encourage mayhem or maliciousness on the court, but the lasting satisfactions of doubles at its best.

SERVER—LEAD THE POINT . . . OR LOSE IT

As the server, you hold the fate of the game in hand as surely as you hold the tennis ball you are about to toss. Your job is to take advantage of this position of great leverage by serving with shrewdness and skill, and then moving up to the service line to back up your serve with an accurate first volley.

Before all else, you must develop the consistency in your serving that permits you to get the first serve in most of the time. You will be convinced of the validity of this familiar doubles dictum the first time you yourself face a server who never or almost never commits a fault. The pressure and frustration your team will experience in trying to break service will be great.

The reason for building consistency rather than brilliance, or a high percentage of aces, into your first serve in doubles is simple: It forces the receiver to stand in a deep and neutral position, unsure of where you are going to place the serve and of what designs your partner may have on the return. The receiver's ambition is limited to getting the ball back crosscourt and low. That gives your partner a chance to poach.

If you fault on the first serve, however, the situation changes drastically. The receiver now can move up inside the court with the knowledge that, on your second serve, you will be forced to serve not only

((33))

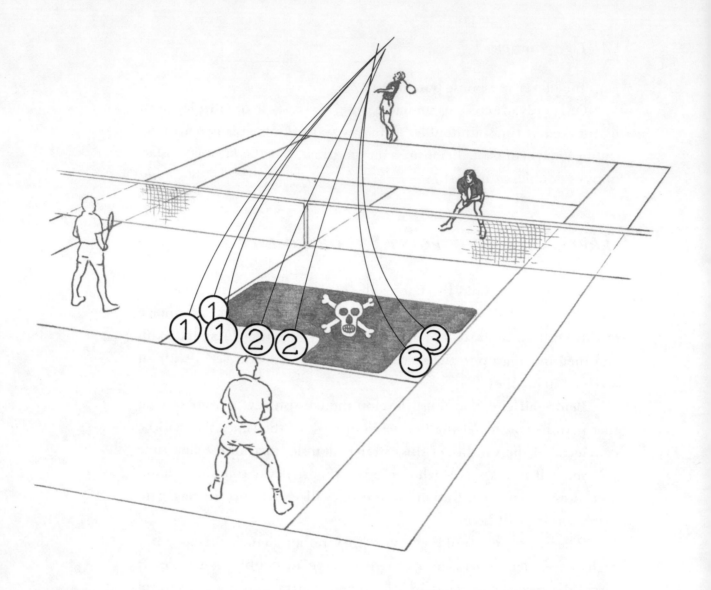

SERVER

The server's main job is to get the first serve in to maintain the team's offensive edge. Your bread-and-butter serve is to the opponent's weaker or backhand side—No. 1 in the illustration, which presumes that the receiver is righthanded. Option 2 is to hit right at him, hoping to jam his stroke on the return, and Option 3 is to hit an extreme slice to the forehand side to pull him off the court. Options 2 and 3 are basically change-of-pace serves. Any serve falling short of the desired landing areas is vulnerable to attack by the receiver.

with less pace but with less variety. Chances are the opponent will be able to anticipate exactly the type of ball you hit, and thus will be able to step into the return quickly and aggressively. Your partner, also fully aware you are going to have to serve with less pace and variety, will have had to give up on any poaching ideas and retreat a step or two to protect against a possible hard return down the line. That, in turn, opens up more of your side of the court for attack, so that the receiver may be free to hit past you down the middle.

The distinct strategic disadvantages that come out of having to resort often to a second serve also work definite psychological changes. Your confidence is bruised, and your partner feels he or she is playing under extra duress. Even worse, the opponents become undeservedly buoyed up and in an offensive frame of mind.

A consistently "good" first serve—good in the sense that it gets over the net and hits in the service box—must also have depth and variety in its placement before it's good in the sense of being effective in doubles.

To prevent the receiver from stealing the offensive, you must get your serve in deep—at the least within a yard of the service line and, against first-rate returners, within a *foot* of the line. A deep serve, even if it lacks speed, will generally keep any receiver back after hitting the return. Bear in mind that an excess of speed on the serve can actually hurt you, in giving you less time to move in behind it.

To prevent the receiver from using a favored ground stroke—forehand or backhand—you must be able to consistently direct your serve not only deep but to the player's weaker side as well. Then, to prevent anyone's becoming grooved and increasingly effective on that weaker side, you must slip in occasional serves wide to the player's strong side, or occasional deep serves right at the player, to change the pace and, with the shots into the body, to jam the stroke.

SERVER—FIRST VOLLEY

Following a good serve, the server must move in to a balanced position near the service line to await the receiver's return. The first volley should be played safely back into the direction from which it came, deep if the receiver has stayed back, more shallow if he has rushed in. Your goal is to place the ball around his feet to force him to hit a weak, low volley or half-volley back.

It is vital to experiment in keeping your opponent honest, but don't experiment foolishly. The best time to serve to the opponent's strong side, for instance, is when you are ahead 40—0 or 40—15, and *not* when you are behind 15—30 or 30—40.

Again, the reason we are emphasizing depth and accuracy in your serving is to give the receiver a minimum of preparation time, a narrow range of possible types of shots to hit on the return, and a small area to hit back to with safety. If you can consistently create these conditions, an opponent will rarely give you much trouble. If not, you—and especially your partner—will pay the price.

As the server, you should stand at the baseline at a point approximately midway between the center line and the doubles sideline. That is quite a bit farther over from the usual serving position in singles, which is right next to the center line. The wider serving position facilitates moving into the court following your serve, to a point that will allow you to cover the range of possible returns by the receiver. In particular, it protects against the wide crosscourt return which is the receiver's most likely return anyway. In effect, you serve and then move to the center point of the court area which is most likely to come into play on the return. Serving from the singles position, you would have to take several additional steps to get to the same place, by which time any reasonably good crosscourt return would be past you.

This serving position may vary according to the court you are hitting to, the weaknesses of certain receivers, the type of serve you are hitting, and other special conditions that sometimes dictate unusual serving tactics. We'll explain how and why such variations come into play later on.

Because as a good server in doubles, you must commit yourself not just to serving the ball well, but to trying to volley the opponent's return, let's for the moment stick to the importance of the server's moving

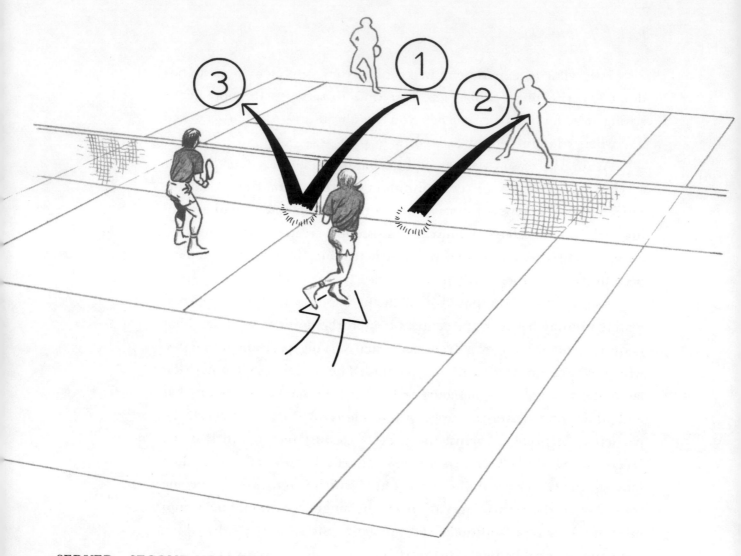

SERVER—SECOND VOLLEY

Following a deep first volley, the server must continue to advance on the net to maintain the pressure of attack. Look for a chance to volley more aggressively this time, either down the middle of the court toward the receiver's backhand, directly at the opposing net player to force a mistake, or wide to the sideline to end the point. Options 2 and 3 are more viable off high balls.

from that position *forward* into the court following serve.

You will find, if you are of average quickness, that you will be able to get through no man's land—the area between baseline and service line—in time to set up to volley most returns. The distance is eighteen feet, but if you have served properly you will have stepped into the court on your follow-through and given yourself a head start toward your objective.

Actually, you can come up short of the service line by a couple of steps and still be in position to volley effectively, depending on the return. We're really only asking you to scamper across the equivalent of a kitchen floor of average size, and then stop and set up for your volley.

Moving in following serve is not the major track event that many club players take it to be. To these players, "rushing net" means running headlong for the net and not stopping until they get there. You can literally run into an opponent's return if you try to get too far into the court, and be forced to volley in a jammed or awkward position. Or you can be passed completely, by a well-placed soft return down the middle or in your alley, or by a surprise lob.

From a stable ready position at or near the service line, your first volley should be made deep back to the receiver if the return is low, or at or past the opposing net player if the return is weak and high— if it's a floater. Against the more common low return that has been chipped back to you, you must concentrate on keeping the ball in play, away from the reach of the opposing net player, and deep to the receiver's feet. Then you must move in another step or two to firmly establish your control of the net, and to wait in anticipation of making a more aggressively angled second volley that, at least in a textbook exchange, will win the point for you outright.

Don't forget, as the server in doubles, that your job is both to serve *and* to volley. Having got an effective first serve in to the receiver's weak side, to continue to control the point you must move into position to play a safe first volley back to the receiver, and then, if necessary, move in even closer to play a more aggressive second volley.

Whenever it's your turn to serve in doubles, try to feel that you are running the show. We're not suggesting you walk up to the line with a too jaunty or unrealistic confidence in your abilities. But do show some enthusiasm for the attack. This is at the core of the serving responsibility in doubles. Too often players go up to serve in a tentative or passive manner, instead of assuming the leadership qualities the role naturally requires.

SERVER'S PARTNER—JACK-IN-THE-BOX AT NET

As the server's partner, your main job is to support the pattern of play of the server, by attacking all weak returns and protecting your side of the court against any strong returns, or the lob.

We cannot stress too much the need to be on your toes in this role at net. There is nothing more ineffectual in tennis than the net player whose feet are set in concrete, or who is too timid to step into the attack or to defend his or her alley with enthusiasm. The server's partner must be a jack-in-the-box to do this job well.

Keep your eyes forward—on the receiver—so that you can react immediately to what he or she does with the return. Never mind watching your own partner—there's nothing to be gained by studying his serving form; in fact you would lose a split second of anticipation each time. And whether you are staring at your partner in derision or admiration, you risk affecting *his* concentration at a crucial moment.

Instead of watching the server, watch the serve. See where the ball

SERVER'S PARTNER—OFFENSIVE ROLE

The job of the server's partner at net is to make a strong serve stronger, by poaching or threatening to poach, and to dig into a sound defensive position when the need arises, as on weak second serves or when the receiver chooses to lob on return. In the latter case the net player must scoot back and play an overhead.

is landing and step in the direction of the likely return.

You should stand in an alert ready position at about dead center in the service box. That puts you close enough to net to step in and volley aggressively, yet far enough back to field any lobs the receiver attempts to throw over your head, while still being close enough to the sideline to keep the receiver from hitting a winner down the line off your partner's serve—especially a wide serve. You are also close enough to the center line to cross and poach.

As a rule, the better your partner's serve, the closer you may stand to the net with impunity and, theoretically at least, the easier it will be for you to cross and intercept returns. However, the skill of the returner must also be weighed before deciding to stand in any extreme position within the service box. For instance, you would naturally play deep against an expert at the lobbed return of serve.

You want to stand close enough to the net to hit high volleys—but not so close that you don't have time to see the ball—or that you can't fully cover your half of the court. Better players generally can stand farther back and still be effective, as they have confidence in hitting the low volley.

Your job as server's partner is to both protect and to threaten. In this position in particular, the latter role is often the more effective. An offense based on effective poaching can quickly develop into an impregnable defense.

It does not matter how often you poach, or even if you poach successfully every time you try it. The important thing is to be on the verge of poaching at every opportunity, in order to force the returner to worry about you as well as think about receiving serve. Often, such added pressure will win your side easy points, as the receiver, losing concentration and security, hits returns into the net or wide down the line. But if you seldom or never poach, the receiver will quickly become grooved in a crosscourt return pattern that will let him develop the confidence to make passing shots at your expense.

Good poaching can salvage a game when the server is not producing shots with his or her usual zip and accuracy. If you can win a point outright by poaching after your partner has hit a weak or indifferent serve, you may boost the server's sagging spirits and get a wayward serve back on track.

To provide the most support for the server, you must learn to poach spontaneously and by design, and occasionally to fake poaching as well.

In spontaneous poaching, you move to cut off a return because you see that the ball is going to cross the net near the center with a lot of clearance or at a rate of speed that will give you time to get there and put it away. You should aim a put-away volley for the open court between your two opponents, or directly at the opposing net player who, generally, will be fairly helpless to return.

In poaching by design, you decide to intercept a return before the point has begun. You might make it conditional on the serve bouncing to the receiver's more vulnerable backhand side, but basically you are "premeditating" the act. You should be in motion just before or exactly at the moment the receiver makes contact with the ball.

Your timing must be precise when you are poaching by design. If you move too early, the receiver has time to alter his or her stroke and drill the return down your unprotected alley. If you move too late, your partner will have to play the shot with both of you in the same half of your court.

You must also be prepared to cope with the unexpectedly weak return that you actually overrun. You find yourself forced to try to hit the ball with your backhand volley rather than the forehand volley you had carefully groomed for the occasion. Sometimes the return will be

((43))

SERVER'S PARTNER—DEFENSIVE ROLE

When the server has missed first serve, the net player must immediately prepare to shield himself and his lane from a hard offensive return. There is an outside chance that he will have to retreat to lob back an offensive lob, but his main concern will be "reflexing" a volley back in order to keep his side in the point.

too good and you simply won't be able to reach it. In that case, just try to get out of the way of your partner as he or she makes a pass at it.

You'll stretch your poaching effectiveness, and increase confusion and uncertainty in the receiver, if you also *pretend* to poach from time to time, by starting across or toward the net a step or two or merely by faking with head and shoulders, and then quickly resuming your ready position. Such sudden moves will distract the receiver, and occasionally they will actually fool the opponent into returning to your side, productive of balls which you should be able to volley away smartly.

Whenever you poach, do it with gusto. You are in motion for one reason: to attack and end the point, win or lose. Half-hearted poaching gets the ball back over the net, but with your own team's defenses in shambles.

If the server fails to get the first serve in, you will have to concentrate on protecting yourself and your alley, but don't forget about poaching as so many club players do at this point. If the receiver knows for sure you will not poach, he or she will be able to play the return with increased confidence. On the second serve, you should stand back a step or two until you see what kind of serve your partner hits, and what the return is like. Your first concern is the possibility of a strong return—a big backhand or a runaround forehand—down the line or right at you. If the return goes crosscourt, your concern becomes a possible poach by the opposing net player, who will be looking to intercept any weak shot by your partner, and to volley it past you or low at your feet. In either circumstance, you are definitely in the hot seat and must concentrate solely on staying alert, relaxed, and ready to trust your reflexes to keep your side in the point.

For all its perils, the cold-blooded poach is the guts of the job of server's partner at net. If in the opponent's mind there is the ever-present danger of poaching, the efficiency on returns is certain to diminish. If you don't make the receiver aware of your presence—as someone who is ready, willing, and able to poach—then you might as well sit down, at least early in the point, because your initial usefulness to the team will be nil.

RECEIVER—FIGHTING OUT OF THE CORNER

Most doubles matches are won, not on the basis of glorious serves, as in singles, but on crafty, dogged service returns.

Receiving serve demands the greatest amount of concentration of all four basic doubles roles, because you must react spontaneously to a prepared attack in conditions that strongly favor the other side. Not until the return is completed can your partner so much as lift a finger to help you in any way. So, in the few seconds it takes for you to receive and return, you are actually playing alone against two. Skilled opponents will make you feel that pressure thoroughly.

Your *frame of mind* for the return of serve must be as highly concentrated as it is for the serve. This takes more of an effort, because you are not initiating the action. There is also the hazard of the opposing net player who moves around a lot, feinting and darting around, poaching or threatening to poach. It is easy to take your eye off the ball and your mind off the point amid such goings-on.

Planning what you are going to try to do with the return, even before the ball is served, is a good way to focus your mind on the play. Leave your instincts to cope with unexpected developments—such as a surprise slice serve to your forehand, or the net man actually crossing in looking for a poach—and try to plot your response according to the likely serve.

Even the position you assume for receiving must of necessity be

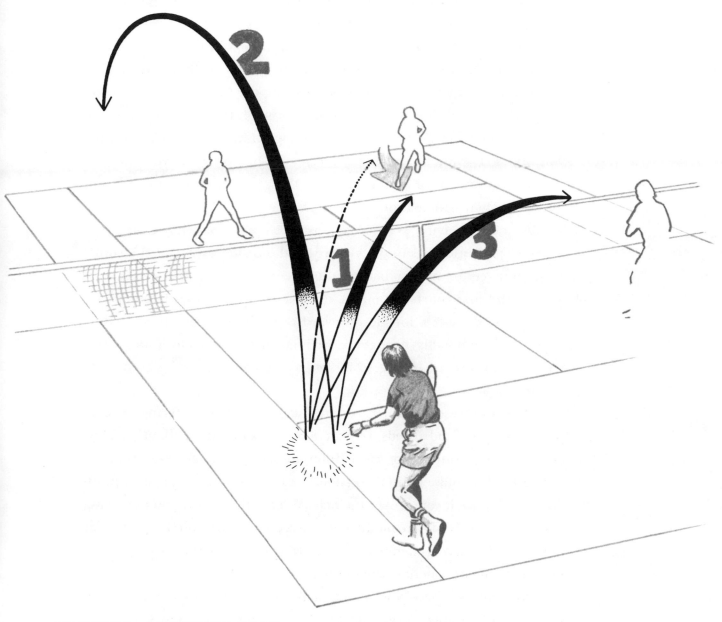

RECEIVER—DEFENSIVE ROLE

Against a strong serve, the receiver's No. 1 option is to chip a backhand crosscourt to the server's feet, whether the server rushes in or hangs back at the base line. Option No. 2 is the deep lob down the line, effective as a change of pace or even used more regularly if the serve is really tough to handle. A third option is a dink shot played short and wide.

an insecure one because, against versatile servers, you are never sure where the ball is going to land. Some players stand a couple of feet behind the baseline, others at the line, still others inside. The depth at which you stand to receive serve depends mainly on how much pace the server usually hits with. The point along the baseline at which you stand varies according to your anticipation of the type of serve the opponent is going to try next, or a feeling about what kind of return you yourself want to try. Many players also like to move sideways, forward, or backward at the moment the serve is struck in order to maximize their anticipation.

A good receiving position against the opponent who serves from a standard position lies in the vicinity of the inside corner of the court, with your feet on or just behind the baseline.

In the first court you might stand a bit more toward center and in the second court a bit more toward the side, in order to give your forehand, presumably stronger, a greater chance to come into play— without, however, standing so far over that you risk being aced wide to the forehand.

The variety of styles in serving, arising out of differing serving positions, spins, and speeds, require that you establish a slightly different receiving position for each different server. In all cases, though, the basic idea holds: Be in a position from which to get your best jump on the ball once it comes over the net. Observe the results you're getting and always be ready to modify your receiving position by a step or steps in any direction, until you know you are in the best spot for meeting your opponent's usual effort.

No matter where you stand, make sure you adopt a balanced, active, catlike stance. Keep weight off your heels, position your head and your racket forward, and glue your eyes to the ball as the server lifts it in the toss. Each individual act of readiness intensifies your concentration and contributes to quicker reactions.

Now let's consider the actual return. As receiver, your main job is to minimize the built-in advantages of the serving side, and at your first opportunity to seize the offensive and move into net.

The first half of this job depends entirely on your return. To keep the opponents from running away with the point, you must get the serve back so that (1) the opposing net player is unable to cross, poach and crack the ball through your partner, and (2) the server, rushing in, is unable to volley down on your return, either deep to you, which would push you back into an even more defensive posture, or hard at or past your partner.

The best approach to keeping the opposing net player out of the picture is to hit crosscourt returns of serve that are sufficiently low and angled to prevent the net player from reaching them—unless that player chooses to cross. To defend against the consequences of such crossing, you as receiver must also be able to hit surprise lobs off the return, plus shots down the line, otherwise the net player might begin to cross and poach at will. By producing a variety of returns, you can make the net player become edgy and indecisive and of little help to the server.

The best approach for keeping an aggressive server from moving in and hitting point-winning volleys off your returns is to hit the bulk of your returns so that the ball skims the net on a low trajectory and lands near the server's feet. This chipped return—"chipped" because the stroke is a sawed-off version of the normal ground stroke—is the mainstay stroke for the good receiver. When engineered well, it forces the onrushing server to hit a low volley or a half-volley (a ball that has just bounced) and so prevent that player from sending the ball back low and hard. Rather, the player may have to scramble back a high ball that you will be able to move in on yourself.

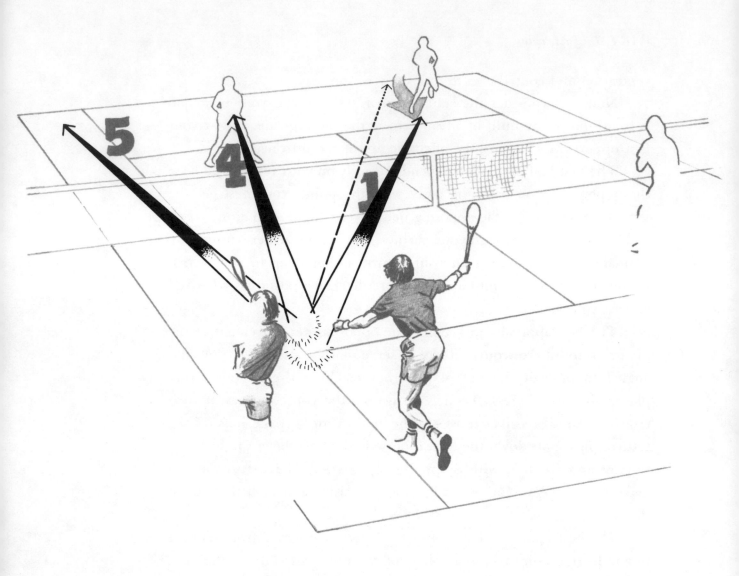

RECEIVER—OFFENSIVE ROLE

Any weak serve that can be attacked, especially on the forehand side, expands the receiver's options to include hard returns at the net player or down the line, (Options No. 4 and No. 5). Option No. 1 here is a more aggressive version of the basic crosscourt backhand return, hit flat or even with topspin if that is within your capability.

It is by returning skillfully back to an aggressive server that you are most likely to obtain the offensive when starting from a receiving position. The deep returns of first serve that are common in singles will usually get you nowhere in doubles, because the ball will be crossing the net at a height of four or five feet—high enough for perhaps either opponent to volley down on. You can't prevent a server from moving in following his or her serve, but you can make that first volley position awkward for the player, and that must be your limited objective. So chip accurately until you have whittled down the advantage with which the opposing team began the point. Then move into net on the first short or high ball, or when the opponents have retreated, and force the issue with more offensive shots and some fast volley action in close.

The receiver has a duty to ruthlessly exploit weak second serves. But to do this, you must quickly adjust your thinking from first serve to second serve. Instead of chipping safely, you must move in for the kill, either by running around your backhand and drilling a forehand at the server or the net player, or by coming over the ball in a full backhand that keeps the server back. Not only will this aggressive approach on second serves win you some "easy" points but it will shake up the confidence of both opponents.

The weak second serve is a serious weakness in the server. Not taking advantage of it is an even more serious mistake for the receiver.

RECEIVER'S PARTNER—WATCHDOG IN WAITING

This is the least active of the four roles in doubles and in some ways the most vulnerable role on the court, at least in the early stages of any point. Your job as receiver's partner is to support the pattern of play

RECEIVER'S PARTNER—DEFENSIVE ROLE

If the net player's partner hits a weak return, the player at net is likely to be the target of any one of several aggressive shots by the opposing team. The opposing net player may poach on the return, or the server may come in and hit a hard first volley off the return. All the receiver's partner can do is try to block back any hard volleys hit at him. If the return is wide, he must beware of the server attacking his alley.

created by your partner in making the return, but that is no cinch. Since the typical return will be defensive rather than offensive, the first danger you face is the opposing net player, and specifically that player's poaching on your partner's return and attempting to volley through you or between you and your partner.

This danger remains even when the opposing net player fails to poach on the return, for, if the serve then hits a good deep first volley, your partner will have to return defensively again, perhaps even more weakly, and thus invite poaching for sure, or maybe an aggressive second volley by the server at you or past you.

Where you stand in the court reflects the defensive nature of your role as receiver's partner. To protect as well as possible against poaching, you must stand farther back in the court than the opposing net player, at least during the first couple of exchanges on the point. A position on the service line near the center of the court will approximate the middle point in the range of possible poached shots off your partner's return by the opposing net player. You'll be back far enough to have the moment's extra anticipation you will need to get your racket on such a shot. Here you will also be in good position for calling the serve, a necessary function of the receiver's partner in club play. But don't play linesman to the detriment of your real job. Switch your focus as soon as you can to the server and the server's partner, and your reactions will be quicker.

On second serve, you may move a couple of steps closer to net if you expect your partner to return serve with an aggressive shot. In this case, you may have the opportunity to poach on the server's riposte, particularly if the server has not moved in from the baseline following serve.

You must make an extra special effort to stay alert in the role of receiver's partner. Like the good watchdog, you never know when

RECEIVER'S PARTNER—OFFENSIVE ROLE

If your partner returns well on first serve, you should be alert yourself to poaching on a weak first volley or half-volley by the server coming in. Watch out for volleys blocked back at you by the opposing net player especially if your partner likes to run around short serves and cream forehands down the line.

you may have to spring into action, but you must be ready to react at a moment's notice to do any good at all. One good way to develop maximum attentiveness in this spot is to make note of the type of return your partner has made, and the reactions of the opponents.

You can often determine what to expect on a point by observing the height at which your partner has returned the serve. If the return is high, count on the next shot being hit down at you, either by the server rushing in or by the server's partner crossing and poaching, and be ready to back up a step or two and try to get your racket on the ball with your reflexes and a bit of luck. If the return is low, count on the next shot going back to your partner, and be ready to step forward and poach yourself if the shot floats high or slow. If the return is a lob, immediately retreat to join your partner at the baseline, in anticipation of the overhead.

The moves of your opponents in response to the return also will tip you off to what's coming and provide you with that extra fraction of a second for preparing to volley or otherwise improving your position. Remember, you are close enough to the net to send the ball back quickly enough to befuddle the opponents, if you have the luck and the reflexes to carry it off. You're also a prime target for the opponents in your position as receiver's partner, but that knowledge should only add to your satisfaction when you do hang in there and get a piece of the action.

STAYING BACK FOLLOWING SERVE OR RETURN

It would be unrealistic for us to expect you to be able to rush net on every point, no matter how energetic, ambitious, and skilled you may be. In fact, such an approach is not even good strategy, in that your pattern of play would quickly become predictable. So before we go any further, let's examine the principal variations in play which emerge when you do not move in following serve or return, and what your responsibilities become under these conditions.

If you stay back as server or receiver, your main job is to assume a ready position at a point in your part of the backcourt which you judge to be at about the center of the range of possible crosscourt shots hit back at you. Thus, if you have served or returned wide, you would move a step or two nearer your sideline in anticipation of the wide shot back. If you have served or returned short and your opponent is moving in on the ball, you would take a step or two behind the baseline in order to field the deep shot the opponent will be trying to hit at your feet. If you have made a deep crosscourt return yet elect to stay back, you should move behind the baseline if you see the opponent moving in to volley the shot, or step a few feet into the court if you see that the opponent also is staying back.

It is vital to quickly get into a good hitting position when you stay back, in order to be ready to go on the attack should the opportunity present itself. While you have not seized the initiative on the point by staying back, neither have you necessarily surrendered it, in that, should the opponent hit a short crosscourt return or a weak volley, you can move in on it aggressively. Otherwise, you can at least make a solidly defensive crosscourt return, or possibly throw up a lob over the head of the opposing net player.

Too many players turn passive when they remain at the baseline following serve or return, not realizing that a steady crosscourt pattern of shots or a surprise lob can maneuver one of the opponents out of position or force a careless shot. You must be alert to exploit such developments before the opponents recover. And don't forget that you can move up to net behind your shot in these circumstances just as you would do following an aggressive first serve.

When a point continues to develop beyond the first few exchanges, the four basic doubles roles blur somewhat. Depending on what has happened in the rally, your team finds itself either up at net or back at the baseline. What are the general responsibilities of the players in these situations?

NET PLAY DURING POINT IN PROGRESS

Your general role at net during a rally is to try to create and then exploit an opportunity to hit down on a ball and sweep it to an open corner, or down the middle, or directly into the body of one of the opponents for the winner. To do that you must remain very conscious of keeping your eye on the ball and alert to the danger of letting up even slightly on any shot that you execute. You are in a favorable position, but a tenacious team will keep the ball in play unless you thoroughly and decisively take command. Keep your racket up, feet lively, eyes intently following the action of the point and the flight of the ball. Be ready to step back to handle any lob and to step forward into each volley, and always hop back into a lithe, ready stance.

BACKCOURT PLAY DURING POINT IN PROGRESS

When you and your partner have been forced to the baseline, your main job is to try to stay in the point—to survive. You should hit defensive lobs to maintain a holding pattern; or lobs behind which you may be able to come to net and regain the initiative; or try to drill ground strokes in between your opponents, preferably with lots of topspin, in an effort to provoke indecision and error on their parts. If you can get them both to commit themselves to going for the ball, you may force a racket error—and at the least you will open up the sidelines for your next shot.

PART II

Tailoring Your Strokes to Doubles

CHAPTER 4

Serve with Spin at Three-Quarter Pace

WE HAVE OUTLINED the basic principles of modern doubles, and the varying roles that doubles players must learn to perform in the course of a match. Now we must examine the strokes and shot-making skills that are part and parcel of good doubles play.

After all, it is not enough just to have a sound strategic approach to doubles. In our opinion, discussion about doubles is too often limited to this area when clearly it is also vital to have the *tools* with which to put your knowledge and strategy to work.

For example, it does little good to come into net following your serve—in implementing one of the cardinal strategies of doubles—if you don't have the technical know-how to execute a sound first volley. It may be a good way to get battle-hardened, as we suggested earlier, but it would be far better for you to have your weapons ready before the battle is joined.

((61))

So let's now leave the chalkboard of doubles theory and get out onto the practice court. Here we will glance at each major stroke in tennis and try to pinpoint its particular value and purpose for doubles. At the same time, we'll suggest some shortcuts to tailoring your own basic tennis strokes so that you will be able to make the shots that are the means for implementing winning doubles tactics.

The controlled and consistent serve that is indispensable to doubles is within range of all tennis players. It takes a certain amount of patience and practice to develop the serve to the point where you can rely on it nine times out of ten—as you must in order to impress and eventually oppress your opponents with your relentlessly good first serve. But, once you have grooved the serve, it will be a permanent part of your game that rarely goes out of whack. The ideal doubles serve requires less precise timing than the all-out, flat, fast serve that is the calling card of some of the top pros, because the racket is in contact with the ball for a longer interval, thus providing greater spin and control. That is why it can become so reliable.

The basis of the doubles serve is a relaxed arm and a racket action that imparts a high degree of spin to the ball when it is hit.

Too many players hurl themselves at the ball when serving, similar to a baseball pitcher rearing back to deliver a scorching fast ball, instead of swinging the arm at a smooth 70–80 percent of capacity rate, in the manner of the control pitcher who catches a corner of the plate with his curve. There really is no need to exert yourself excessively on the serve, either in singles or in doubles. Not only will this practice fatigue you rapidly, but it will tend to breed kinks and contortions in your service motion, none of which add to the speed or power of the serve no matter what you may think they are adding. If you want to prove this to your-

GRIP RACKET FOR MAXIMUM SPIN

It is crucial in doubles to develop a consistent, well-placed first serve; control, rather than speed, should be your main consideration. If you have a standard Eastern forehand grip, turn your hand to the left (for a righthander) until you can see all four knuckles, as you look down on the grip in your service-ready position. If you use this for serving, the racket face will come into the ball more obliquely and thus impart greater slice or twist spin, with no special exertion of wrist or elbow on your part.

self, try serving with no body motion whatsoever sometime—relying solely on your arm and wrist snapping the racket into the ball—and you will see that last-minute action is what generates the bulk of the power in serving, and not the Waltz of the Toreadors that so many players seem to go through every time.

Approach the serve in a relaxed manner, and you'll be more likely to swing at a smooth, three-quarters tempo. Breathe deeply a couple of times as you go to the line, especially if it's in your nature to rush things or be nervous. Hold your racket in your free hand, not your gripping hand, until you get to the line, and when you finally do take hold of the racket, grip it lightly. Bounce the ball a few times to sustain the relaxed air. Toss the ball with a long, smooth arm-lift to set a rhythmical pattern for the other arm to follow. And *watch* the ball until you feel your racket make contact—that will prevent you from lunging into the serve at the last second.

How do you develop the racket action that imparts the spin to the ball that we have said is so desirable in serving in doubles? The simplest way to learn the feel of different racket actions is by varying the position to which you toss the ball initially.

Let us assume you are standing at the baseline in the first court, ready to serve for doubles. If you toss the ball away from you toward the net, you will hit the ball by bringing the racket directly into the back of the ball and up through the point of contact in the direction of your target. This flat serve will fly straight and low at your target, clearing the net by little more than a foot. When it bounces, it will tend to bounce low, depending on the surface, because the ball is spinning end over end.

If you toss the ball away from you *toward the sideline,* you will hit it by bringing the racket *around* the side of the ball and through the point of contact somewhat to the right of your target. The resulting slice serve will fly in a fairly sharp diagonal toward your target, at a slower rate of speed than the flat serve, clearing the net by two or three feet. When it hits, it will tend to bounce low and in the direction of the *sidespin* that has been imparted to the ball. It can be directed to any part of the court.

If you toss the ball directly *above your head,* you will hit it by bringing the racket under the ball, then across the back of the ball from bottom to top at an angle up and slightly away from you. The racket will carry up through the point of contact, and somewhat to the right of target. This kick or twist serve will fly straight, also at a slower rate of speed than the flat serve, clearing the net by several feet and then dropping sharply in trajectory due to the topspin that has been imparted to the ball. When it hits, it will tend to bounce up and "kick" sharply to the right (for right-handers), in the same direction as the sidespin that has been imparted to it.

So far as doubles is concerned, the two significant facts in this comparison of the three basic serves in tennis are the amount of clearance over the net that each serve provides, and the relative speed at which each serve travels.

The slice and twist serves clear the net with two to four feet to spare—a considerably greater margin for error than the flat serve. These serves, once grooved, thus fulfill that prime responsibility of the server mentioned earlier of providing a high percentage of good first serves.

These two serves also take longer to reach their destination because the added spin on the ball elongates their flight pattern. That extra time gives you the chance to follow the shot into net—your second responsibility as server—and also to set yourself up properly for making your first volley. By contrast, an all-out flat serve against a good receiver may come back to you so fast that you are still in motion, forcing you

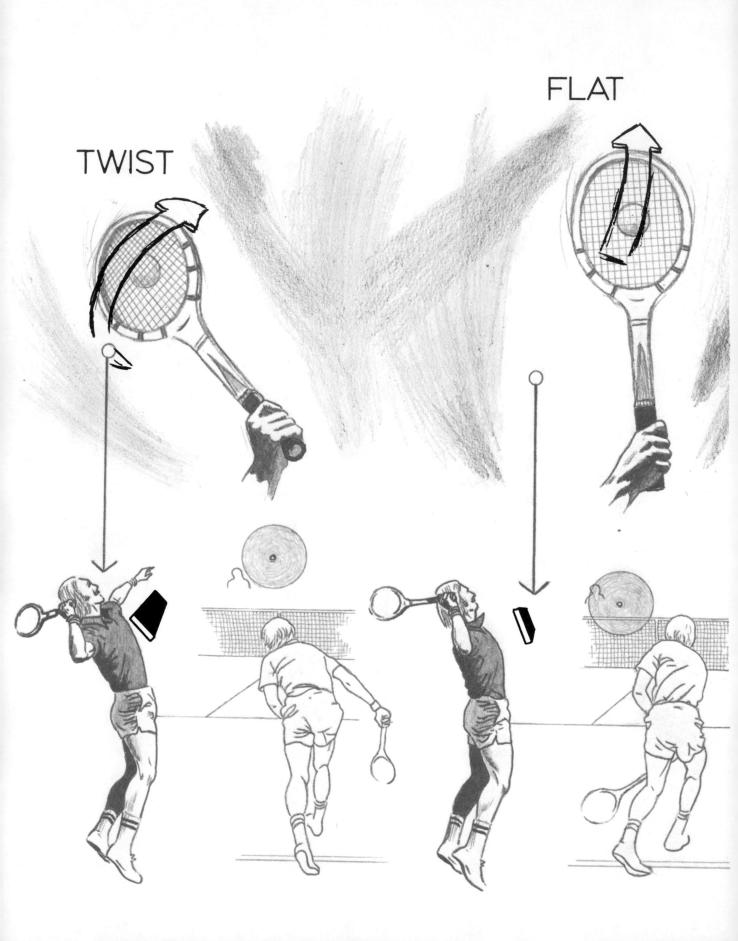

SLICE

VARY SERVES TO FOOL OPPONENTS

Mastering a twist, flat, and slice serve all at once may be easier said than done, but there is no denying that having access to all three distinctly different serves is a great asset in playing doubles. Note the variations in ball toss, shoulder alignment, and wrist-and-racket action occasioned by the three basic serves. Also note the relatively high clearance of the ball over net in the twist and slice serves, compared to the flat serve. The spin serves not only fly into the net less often, they also give the server more time to advance into the court and get in position for a sound first volley. That's why they are recommended for doubles.

to hit the volley off balance if you hit it at all.

The three extremes in serve can be achieved by the better player with much less variety in the position to which the ball is tossed, which would help to keep the receiver in the dark about your intentions. But tossing to these extremes is a good way to get a feeling for the types of racket-on-ball behavior that are mechanically possible in tennis. Once you have become familiar with the range of serves, you should develop a ball toss that does *not* vary substantially, not only to insure maximum deceptiveness in your serving, in the long run, but to enable you in the long run to develop a grooved serving motion. Tossing the ball all over the place will develop chaos in your serve, not consistency.

Once you have standardized your ball toss, you will gravitate towards developing either a slice or a twist serve. Don't try to impede this natural development by reintroducing great variety in the toss, or by seeking an extreme version of the type of serve you seem to be repeating most often. It is vital that you let your natural serve emerge, because that is the one you will be able to groove more comfortably and play with under match pressure with the greatest dependability.

Beware of tossing the ball too near to yourself for either spin variation. Remember, your serving motion should naturally bring you into the court as the racket makes contact with the ball. If you are not stepping forward automatically with the serve, start tossing the ball farther inside the court.

Also, bear in mind that an extreme twist serve causes wear and tear on all but the strongest backs. In fact, its name derives from the manner in which you must corkscrew your spine in order to hit up and through a ball that has been tossed to a spot directly over your head.

To a certain extent you will be able to modify your natural spin in favor of the other spin, when circumstances dictate, simply by aiming at the spot in the opponent's court where the change-of-pace serve would tend to hit. Your target projection will automatically dictate slight changes in your toss, body movement into the ball, and wrist-and-racket action to produce the desired serve.

For example, if you are serving from the first court to a right-hander and you wish to attack the player's backhand by serving down the middle, you will automatically kick it into that corner, by hitting more up on the shot. If it happens that your opponent has a vulnerable forehand, or if you are determined to hit to the player's forehand to change your pattern, you will automatically hit *around* the ball more and slice it wide into the forehand corner. We thus repeat that extreme changes in ball toss or arm swing are not required to produce variation in your serve, once you have a grooved and rhythmic service motion to work with.

There are, however, two seemingly minor points that many doubles players nevertheless tend to ignore in serving. It will not be easy to develop any type of spin serve if you are holding your racket in too much of a forehand grip when serving, or if your racket is strung too tightly for your level of play.

The racket face will come into the ball more obliquely, and thus impart greater slice or twist spin, if you are gripping the handle in something akin to an Eastern backhand or Continental grip. In other words, make sure you turn your hand well over to the left on the handle when serving for doubles. Trying to produce spin on your serves with the forehand grip is not only ineffective, but it strains the elbow, if you're trying to slice the ball, and strains both elbow and back if you're trying to twist it.

Too much racket tension—for most club players that would be anything in the fifty-six-to-sixty-pound range, depending on the string-ing machine—will simply diminish control rather than, as many players think, increase power. The more tightly a racket is strung, the more arm strength you must have to make the racket strings stay on the ball through impact and so provide spin control. Using a racket strung at sixty pounds' tension, which is standard for the pros, is like trying to swing with a stiff board for any club player. It will also send shock waves down your forearm that in time will give you a nasty case of tennis elbow.

It is especially important to be able to put spin on the ball in doubles, not just on the serve but in other shots, such as volleys. One of the all-time great doubles players, John Bromwich of Australia, was noted for playing with a loosely strung racket, so that he had that extra control. Frew McMillan, who with Bob Hewitt constitutes one of the best doubles teams on the circuit today, also swears by low string tension for helping him get maximum "feel."

CHAPTER 5

Chip Your Backhand Returns

IN DOUBLES, the rules give you more court to stand on but less target to hit to. That is especially evident on the return of serve, which in many ways is the finesse stroke of doubles, demanding accuracy and touch far more than the receiving position in singles demands.

As receiver, you are hitting out of a disadvantageous spot to start with—for, if your opponent is worth his salt, he will be serving to your backhand or weaker side most of the time. You have only half the court to return into, for your opponent's partner, if *he* is worth his salt, stands ready to crack any tentative return that strays within his reach. And, finally, you must often contend with the pressure of the server's moving in behind his shot, waiting to volley your return back at you before you have had time to breathe.

Under these circumstances, how can you get the ball back effectively? Generally, the only way to handle good first serves to your backhand is through thoughtfully placed defensive returns. A smooth, sawed-off stroke, more akin to a volley than to a ground stroke, will re-

Alertness in receiving serve counts for a lot. If you can step diagonally in preparing to return serve, rather than sideways, you'll gain a split second in returning the ball. Chances are you will also gain the initiative in the rally.

turn most good serves effectively, provided your body is moving into the return behind a smooth and measured arm-swing. This is the essence of the chipped backhand return.

The difference between blocking and chipping a return is a matter of degree, dictated in the main by the speed of the serve.

"Blocking" the ball back is just a fancy word for sticking your racket in the line of flight. It's your only defense against a very fast serve—and a far better defense than fighting fire with fire by trying to outhit the server. Many players instinctively react in the wrong manner on such shots, taking a big swing against a fast serve instead of trimming the swing in order to meet the ball in front of themselves. The faster the serve, the shorter your backswing should be, to the point that, against extremely fast serves, you are merely punching the serve back, rather like the volley stroke with no backswing at all, attempting to steal the server's speed and send it back in the direction it came.

The chipped return involves a fuller stroke than the blocked return and is used against a serve of moderate pace. It is vital to step into the shot in order to really chip the return, otherwise you risk hitting up on the ball and floating it back high. With your body moving forward, the racket more easily moves through the ball on a downward plane, cutting under the ball and sending it back with underspin.

Many players get into the habit of returning weakly because they fail to step into the shot along the shortest possible path. Club players tend to play sidewise, floating off the court in pursuit of a wide serve rather than moving diagonally to cut it off.

Stepping into the shot with your body on the backhand return is equivalent to stepping into the court in the course of your service motion, in the sense that each movement is integral both to firmness in stroking and to aggressiveness in tactics. When you chip with your weight moving forward, you're better prepared to begin a thrust toward

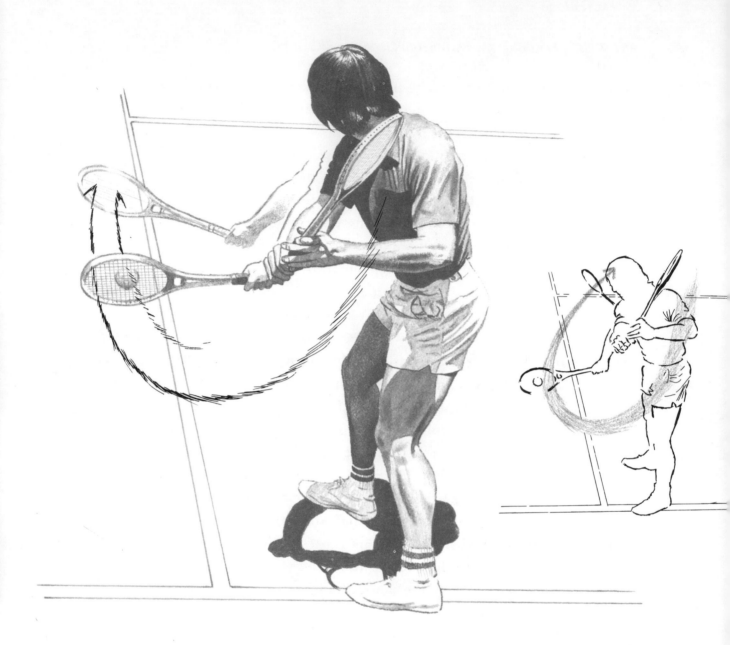

The chipped backhand return of serve is a full stroke, but it is an abbreviated *version of the hard backhand. Note the difference in the length of backswing.*

net if you see your return is finishing near the opponent's net.

It is probably more important to consciously *aim* on your return of serve than on any other single shot in doubles, because the open space you have to work with is so slight. Aiming will also help you to develop the sawed-off stroke you need to return with precision balls hit to your backhand.

Your aiming point for the return depends on what action the server normally takes after hitting the ball. If he is an aggressive player who follows all his serves into net, your aiming point should be about midway on the service line, or just inside the service line. That will automatically shorten your stroke and help you to produce the shallow return that, ideally, will just skim the net and bounce low at the server's feet. Note that such a short ball could invite the player to net in singles play. But in doubles, on the service return at least, it is a fine shot, and usually your best percentage shot.

If your opponent stays back following serve, your aiming point becomes the area just in front of the baseline, to keep him back, and to enable you to come in. In this instance you would probably hit a full stroke, exactly like your crosscourt backhand return in singles. The ball would not necessarily land low at the opponent's feet, since that would require a hard driving shot that just skims the net—too risky for regular use. The chipped short return would not pay off because it would force the opponent to move in to field it. Inadvertently, you would hand over control of the net to the opponent.

The technique of chipping backhand returns requires aiming with concentration and stroking with moderation. It is based on an alert ready position from which you can move diagonally to meet the ball, rather than to the side, so that your body gets *behind* the stroke and insures solid contact. Remember, as receiver it is always better to stand back and move in, rather than stand in and move back.

Many players make the mistake of chopping down on their service returns without backswing or follow-through. Note the smooth downward stroke that imparts backspin to the ball and at the same time is sufficiently long to provide the depth that keeps opponents at bay.

A good ready position also includes the proper grip. If you don't change your grip (as Lutz does not), there is no choice to make. If you do change grips (as Smith does), you should first of all decide what grip to hold the racket with while awaiting the serve. Receiving in the first court, you might stand with the forehand grip, since you should have more opportunities to use the forehand. In the second court you might prefer to wait with your backhand grip, since you will be likely to hit more backhands.

The best approach, however, might be to wait, on either side, with the grip of the stroke that is the *weaker* of the two for you. That way, you will be helping the weaker stroke as much as possible, in that you will be making it easier to be properly prepared for making the stroke on that side.

While the chipped backhand return is the basic stroke to use when receiving against a good server, it may profitably be modified if the opponents are weak in serving, in ways that we will discuss later in dealing with teams of varying characteristics. But, in discussing service return now, we should not omit mention of two important variations to the chipped backhand return that should figure at appropriate times in your defense against teams with serves of any degree of merit. These variations are the runaround forehand and the surprise lob. When blended with a steady chipped backhand return, a receiver's game is strong indeed.

RUNAROUND FOREHAND AND LOB

As a right-hander playing the first court, you should find you have more opportunity to run around balls intended for your backhand side and return them aggressively with your forehand. That is because the angle into your backhand is less generous for the server than it is on the second court.

Since most players can generate more power on the forehand side, this is a great tactic to use against a slow or misplaced serve. It requires quickness afoot and an aggressive forehand, hit at the feet of the server moving in, down the line, or at the net player. If the shot is not aggressive, the opposing net player may cross and volley it into the area of the court you have left vacant by running around.

Running around a weak backhand in the second court is not advisable as standard practice, simply because on that side you would bring yourself well off the court to make the shot. In any case, fewer serves will be hit within range of your forehand in that court.

At the pro level, the surprise lob is seldom employed against a first serve because there just isn't time to set up and execute this delicate touch shot. The defensive lob can and must be used against a really great serve.

At the club level, there may be more opportunities to lob back on first serve. In any case, it is a decidedly useful alternative in returning a second serve, and as a surprise weapon can disrupt your opponents nicely. The art lies in lobbing deep over the net player on the return.

The deep lob return is a more common device on the backhand because (1) if the second serve is directed in range of your forehand, you would probably choose to hit an aggressive forehand instead of lobbing, and (2) it is probably easier for more people to hit the lob with good touch on the backhand side, as we will explain in more detail later on.

CHAPTER 6

Step into More Volleys

THE VOLLEY STROKE—actually it is more of a *shot* than a *stroke*—is at the heart of a versatile game of doubles. Without it, or with some weak or tentative version of it, you will not be able to play doubles to the game's full potential, or to yours. It is a weapon both of attack and defense, surprise and design, and it adds breadth, speed, and excitement to the play.

It also can compensate for whatever limitations you may have in your serve. The great Australian player Ken Rosewall has a relatively weak serve, but his volleying makes up for it. In doubles especially the weakness on his serve means nothing at all, for he has tremendous touch and control on his first volley. His first volley, in effect, adds clout to his serve.

Of all the strokes in tennis the volley is really the least complex, because it is so compact and also because it is executed over such a short interval of time and space. In many situations, you barely have time to make the volley, let alone reflect on it. Yet many players have trouble

((79))

Net play is nearly half the game in doubles. If you wish to play your volley strokes with more authority, you must learn to get your body sideways to the flight of the oncoming ball. The better you can achieve that alignment, the more weight you will be able to deliver to your volley strokes.

acquiring a passable volley stroke. Youngsters exposed to net play from their beginning in the game acquire the volley with ease, because they are comfortable in the situations in which the volley is the ideal shot. But kids who are developed strictly as baseliners, or those who start in the game at more advanced ages, are prone to anxiety near net, and that in itself interferes with the learning process.

The only way to break down the barrier between you and the volley is to plunge into the experience of standing at net and trying to return balls hit at you or near you. A little assertiveness, plus making the eventual discovery that you can survive in the fast and somewhat threatening conditions that exist in the net area, will go a long way toward helping you mentally and emotionally to acquire a sound volley.

Let's examine the technical points to keep in mind in making this important shot work in doubles.

The volley must be made with more accuracy in doubles than in singles simply because, with two opponents instead of one on the other side of the net, your target area is greatly restricted. Lackadaisical "rebound" volleys can be kept in play or put away by the other team.

In order to volley with accuracy, you must execute the shot not just with your arm and hand, but with your shoulders and even your feet. In other words, in order to aim the shot, and so develop accuracy, you must shift your body into position, so that your full thrust takes place in the direction of your target. In making ground strokes you can alter direction by slight changes in wrist action at the last moment, but there isn't time or sufficient length of stroke to do that on the volley. Not only does the accuracy on a volley derive from this body alignment, but so to a certain extent does the power that you generate. The volley stroke itself is so short and quick that it can only use the speed that is on the ball already. However, it can use that speed with more authority if your weight is moving into the shot as you make the stroke.

Ironically, then, on the shot on which you have the least amount of time to do so, moving your feet into position is an action with the greatest impact on the stroke's effectiveness. Hitting volleys with shoulders open and facing the net—with minimal control over where the ball is going—is almost always the result of lazy or just plain tired feet. It's true that in some extremely fast exchanges at net you might "reflex" back volleys without even getting your eyebrows into the shot. But if the effort to move into the shot is not there, even those volleys will not be as sharp and well-directed as they might have been. Usually, there is time to get at least your shoulders around prior to hitting the shot.

Once you are conscious of the value of shifting feet and shoulders into position to direct your volleys, the stroke itself will feel more natural to you. It's a short, punching motion of hand, wrist, and forearm—slightly downward *to* the ball but not significantly *through* it (as on all other strokes)—a motion that ideally puts underspin on the ball, cuts the pace, and keeps it low going back.

You'll be better able to punch your volleys with your feet and shoulders in the stroke if you concentrate on trying to meet the ball off your *front* leg. Once you let a ball get behind you, you will not be able to get your weight into the shot.

This points up a second vital aspect of effective volleying, and that is anticipation. You have more time to prepare to execute any other stroke in tennis, so you can often scramble the ball back if you've been caught napping. For the volley, you must begin to set up for the shot as soon as you see the ball leave the opponent's racket. You have to try to see the ball sooner on the volley simply because you are so close to the net and have less reaction time to work with.

The server's first volley is the prime illustration of the importance of accuracy on this stroke. It has to be directed deep to the returner's feet in order to keep that player in the backcourt. For many players the

((82))

Play all volleys off your front leg. *That assures solid contact and early placement.*

first volley is, unfortunately, the last volley, simply because they don't place it skillfully enough. They either stiff-arm it up to the opposing net player, who takes it for a winner, or bounce it short to the returner, who is free to move in and play an aggressive forehand off it, or even volley back. But if your first volley is accurate, you will be able to move in a few more steps and dominate the play.

Two other elements of good preparation for the volley should be mentioned. First, in moving from serve to first volley, and from first volley to net, don't forget to carry your racket high and in front of you, in a "business" position. And when you move in following serve, be sure to set up in a comfortably balanced stance at or near the service line, rather than standing up straight, or stumbling on toward net.

HIGH VOLLEYS

High volleys—balls reaching you waist-high or above—are usually easier to play than low volleys. But when they look like setups, there is a greater tendency to take your eye off the ball. So watch the "easy" shots with particular sharpness. Resist any temptation to take a wild swing at the easy ball, but do follow through—remember you must generate your own power on this shot. Get your shoulder into the motion. And also bear in mind that you must come *down* with the stroke faster than you would with a volley at waist-level.

A high volley to your backhand side is extremely awkward and may well be the most difficult shot to hit powerfully, so it is important to meet the ball squarely in front of your body rather than think of overhitting and going for too much.

High and low volleys require slight adaptations of your basic technique in handling a ball that comes to you in the air. On high volleys, make sure you follow through more with your racket. On low volleys, be sure to bend your knees so that your hand remains on the same level as your racket head.

LOW VOLLEYS AND HALF-VOLLEYS

Balls hit low to you will be more common the more your level of play rises and the better the players that you face. The key here is to think of bending your legs more, rather than dropping the racket head. Then execute the volley as you normally would.

You will face half-volleys—low balls which you must hit immediately after bouncing—most frequently when your opponent has made a good low return to your feet, or at any time when you are caught in no man's land. As with low volleys, you must bend your knees more than normal to bring your racket down to the level of the shot.

Half-volleys also need to be played with a more deliberate follow through to insure that they will get up and over the net and into the other side of the court with some depth. Many players make the mistake of trapping the ball in their racket strings. If you stroke through it more, you'll be surprised how easy it is to bring it up and keep the ball in play. But don't attempt to play the shot offensively—realize that your opponent has got you in a fix and content yourself with sending the ball back fairly low and in the direction it came from.

The basic technique for all volleys still applies—*see the ball, bend your knees,* and *step into the shot.*

LOB VOLLEY

The lob volley is more properly a lob than a volley but, since it is made when you are at net, we should at least mention it here. It comes into play when all four players are at net intent on keeping the ball low.

The lob-volley is a touch shot, played only when all four players are at net. It can be very effective as a surprise maneuver, but if it fails by an inch, it fails by a mile.

The ball comes to you and you decide to surprise everyone (usually including your partner) by laying back the face of your racket—so that it faces more skyward—and flipping the ball up and over the heads of the opponents. You're not going for a winning lob, but merely trying to force the other team away from the net. Trouble is, if you don't hit the shot just right, it may produce an instant putaway for the opponents. It requires a great deal of touch because you have to take the opponent's speed completely off the shot. But when used judiciously—maybe once every three *matches*—and at a critical point in the play, a successful lob volley is a source of great satisfaction.

CHAPTER 7

Round Out Doubles Arsenal with Lob and Smash

THE LOB AND OVERHEAD, or smash, require substantially the same technical approach for proper execution for doubles as they require for singles. But the two strokes are used with greater frequency in doubles, and for that reason alone we must emphasize the importance of reaching some degree of competence in them, if you really want to learn to play doubles well.

You can play a creditable game of singles without recourse to the lob or overhead, or without much success when you do try them. But in doubles, if you are weak in both strokes you will be at distinct disadvantage—in the same position you would be entering a chess game without your rooks and half your pawns. You are automatically weaker offensively, and thus more vulnerable defensively.

Let's examine both strokes from the point of view of their application in doubles, and with an eye on the technical problems of execution.

((88))

Most players, in singles or in doubles, make the mistake, when lobbing, of shortening their stroke unnecessarily. Try to follow through on the lob as on any shot and you'll discover that you have much more control and greater range of placement.

LOB

A good lob in doubles can have the same effect as dropping a hand-grenade behind your opponents. It can be used for attack, defense, change of pace, or surprise. Employed at the right time, it can get you back into a point you were on the verge of losing, engender confusion and therefore disrupt opposing team morale, or even in a single blow shift the winning momentum in the match to your side.

The lob is invaluable as an alternative on the return of serve, as already mentioned, and also when your opponents have managed to gain control of the net and force your team back to the baseline.

In order to lob accurately, the first thing you must try to do is get set properly. That way you will be able to move forward into the shot for added control and better depth. This is certainly true for the offensive lob, which is a disguised stroke for which you set up and take the racket back as you would for any groundstroke.

But you must frequently use the lob on the run—when you have no time to get set. In scrambling to make such a defensive lob, all you have time to do is get the racket back. You can't *count on* getting power from your body's weight-shift.

The stroke itself involves an ordinary backswing and a forward swing that may be described as a slow-motion version of the forward swing you would use on your ground strokes, in the sense that you are trying to bring the racket strings into the ball in a more deliberate manner in order to increase your feeling for the ball when it strikes. You should definitely have the sensation of "working" the ball rather than hitting it.

Most important is your follow-through. Your racket should move up and through after contact and in the direction in which you are aiming. The lack of any kind of a follow-through accounts for most poor lobs falling short within easy range of the opponents.

There is no significant difference in technique in executing a high defensive lob, as when you are caught out of position and are simply fighting for time to recover, and the lower-flying offensive lob, more commonly used on return of serve as a surprise shot over the opposing net-player's head. If you want simply to hit a low defensive lob, think of stroking the ball in much the same manner as you would for a volley. For a very high lob, think of stroking the ball longer. The differing heights and depths obtained on lobs are entirely a function of stroke length, racket control, and your feel of the ball on the strings.

The topspin lob is a different story. In fact, it requires such good timing and quick wrist action that we would not recommend that any but the most advanced players attempt to develop the shot. It is almost exclusively the province of the forehand side, as the ball must be hit late in order to put the requisite topspin on it, and to hit late on the backhand side puts the ball behind you to an impracticable degree.

For the topspin forehand lob, the racket is held in a slightly cupped position and brought up sharply through the back of the ball in a visible jerky snapping motion. Try to hit it like your forehand, only use more wrist action and flick at the ball at the last moment. When hit correctly, the ball flies over the opponent's head, just out of reach of the player's racket, then drops quickly and bounces off toward the back fence before the opponent can even begin to make a run for it.

To repeat—this is a shot for experts only. The vast majority of tennis players, if they learn to hit ordinary lobs with consistent depth and placement, will never even need a topspin lob to play their best doubles.

The lob has the potential for as much variety in speed and placement as any other stroke in tennis. Make sure you use this shot with the versatility that makes it an especially effective surprise weapon in doubles.

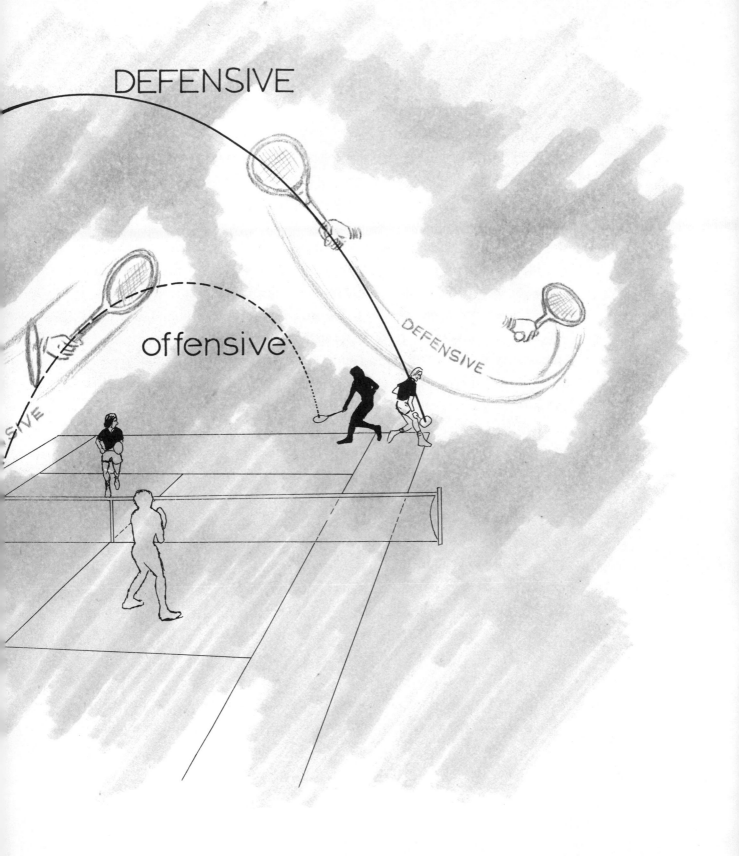

OVERHEAD

The more you play doubles properly—that is, the more you come to net and attempt to stay there—the more you invite some variety of lob by the opponents. Against the lob there is only one sound defense, and that is the overhead stroke.

The overhead—or the smash, as it is called when one is in a more belligerent frame of mind—gives many tennis players trouble mainly because they try to imitate their service motion in executing it.

Possession of a good serve does not insure development of a good overhead. Conversely, if your serve is lousy, it does not exclude the possibility that your overhead will be excellent.

The two strokes, though superficially alike, actually differ in two important ways.

First, in the serve the whereabouts of the target ball is largely controlled by the server. To the extent that you can standardize your toss, you free yourself from the variable of ball location in the course of the serve. In the overhead, no such consistency can be counted on, because you are not controlling the flight. Half the battle is thus getting yourself into the right place in relation to the ball.

The second big difference beween serve and overhead lies in the size of the stroke. There is much less windup involved in the overhead stroke, because setting the ball up and starting your body moving in rhythm is not part of the process, as it must be in the serve to insure maximum coordination among the various moving parts. Players who try to smash a ball by taking a full-scale backswing are not only wasting motion but attempting an extraordinary feat in timing.

The overhead must be reduced to its most elemental components

In doubles, it makes sense to target your overheads on the "T" formed by the lines of the court in-between your opponents, unless one of the opponents is close in to net, in which case you should feel free to target your smash on him.

before it can become a repeating stroke that you can rely on in action.

First, always get into position sideways to the net and far enough back in the court so that the ball is falling in front of you. You want to keep the ball in front of you in order to see it better, and also so that, when the time comes, you'll be able to hit in the center of your racket strings.

At the same time as you move back under the ball, bring the racket into a comfortable position on your shoulder. Never mind looping it or any other fancy maneuver—just fold your arm back so the racket gets into a hitting position in the simplest and most direct manner possible.

The only motion involved in your overhead should be *forward* motion, so swing at the ball while it is still in front of you, aiming to make contact with it while the racket is still moving upward. Most beginners try to get over the ball on the overhead and so hit down on it into the bottom of the net, or miss it altogether. There is also a tendency to hit the ball too late, and thus to make contact too much toward the top of the racket face.

Finally, make sure you complete your hitting motion before you look into the other court. If you're mis-hitting the smash for no apparent reason, concentrate on keeping your head back and your chin up for a split second longer on the swing. That will insure that you're not taking your eye off the ball before you've hit it, and will help you to time your hits better.

If one of the opponents happens to have remained at net while you are winding up for an overhead, use that player as your target. Drilling the overhead at the player's feet will help you to keep from overhitting on the stroke. It will also demoralize your victim, and possibly sow a little discord between the victim and the victim's partner— especially if the partner is the one who set up the overhead in the first place.

If both opponents have retreated, which is the recommended maneuver following a lob, then aim your overhead down the middle. Use the T-shaped intersection of midcourt line and service line as your target, again to prevent overhitting.

When you smash down the middle, the most you can expect from the opponents is a lob hit directly back at you, invariably shorter than the one you've just smashed. You should be able to put this one away by angling at the more convenient open sideline, or battering it between the opponents again.

The topspin lob drops at a considerably faster rate and on a much steeper plane than the conventional lob, because the ball is spinning rapidly end over end; thus, it is harder to judge than a defensive lob.

One of the big problems that intermediate players have on the overhead is failure to get into position to meet the ball in front of their body. Imagine "catching" the ball as though you were playing the outfield in baseball, and you will be back far enough to swing up and through the overhead with sufficient power and control.

Timing must be more precise, because the path of the ball and the path of your racket head will intersect for only a short interval. The paths of racket and a ball hit defensively will coincide longer, because the ball is falling on a flatter, more gradual trajectory.

The overhead is a confidence shot, and the only way to get confidence is through practice and experience. For average players it is probably the last shot to be refined to the point where it can be used effectively in doubles matches. But, until that refinement has occurred, there will be a gap in your play that knowledgeable opponents will learn to exploit by lobbing you mercilessly, to your detriment as a player, and as a partner in a team.

PART III

Keys to a Winning Partnership

CHAPTER 8

Forming a Balanced Doubles Partnership

THE ELEMENTS OF an effective doubles partnership in tennis are many and complex. Games, personalities, and even the backgrounds and offcourt tastes of doubles partners must meet in some congenial manner in order for a smooth working relationship to result on the court.

We are not suggesting that you must seek out an identical twin as partner before you can hope to succeed in doubles. Indeed, two persons in the same mold will rub each other the wrong way on the tennis court as often as two dissimilar persons will get along. The real key to effective teamwork in doubles lies in achieving a balance between the technical skills of the two players, and a reasonable harmony in the emotional relationship. The old cliché that doubles matches are won in the locker room really applies more to the logic of the matchup between partners than to the particular team's choice of tactics for the match.

Remember that you can never win in doubles all by yourself. To a certain extent you can take up the slack if your partner slips into erroneous ways, and certainly a superior player can compensate for some of the weaknesses of an inferior player on his side. But, in doubles, a team of two players of average skill will always beat a team consisting of one player of above-average and one of below-average skill. So you need your partner to win, and you might as well begin appreciating him properly.

It should be mentioned that there have always been players, even among the pros, who are not suited by training or temperament for the game of doubles. They are the ones who insist on hitting booming first serves—and a corresponding increased number of weaker second serves —and burying their service returns in the stands. And they tend to regard their partner as some inferior presence on the court who must be circumvented, belittled, or ignored. Some of these players may actually lack the speed or endurance for singles—but that is the game to which to leave them for the good of all. Even if such a player is your close friend or associate off the court, leave him out of your doubles plans.

But let's confine our remarks to the vast majority of tennis players, who are willing to share the challenge and the fun of the joint effort required by doubles.

Some of the technical and emotional considerations in forming a good doubles team stem from the basic question, *who should play which side?*

It is generally argued that, from a technical point of view, and assuming both players are right-handed, the player with a stronger *forehand* should play the *first* court or forehand side, and the player with the more consistent backhand should play the second court or backhand side. Such an arrangement theoretically sets up the team in its most effective posture for receiving serve, which is so often the deciding factor in a match.

As we shall see, in certain combinations and against certain teams, a more effective arrangement puts the stronger forehand player in the *second* court. But for now, let's examine the merits of the conventional wisdom on matchups, which plays the strong forehand in the first court and the steady backhand in the second court. How do both players then perform?

In this arrangement the first-court player looks for the opportunity to hit offensive shots, especially off second serves, because his forehand can come into play more easily. Paramount is his option of attacking the opposing net player, if the serve is weak enough, by passing him, or hitting through him. In terms of score, he is in the position of having everything to gain and little to lose. If an attempt to go on the offensive at the start of the game should fail, his team is down by only love—15.

The second-court player has fewer opportunities to use his forehand because the opponent can angle his serve to the backhand corner more easily. The second-court player must concentrate on returning the

COVER FOR ONE ANOTHER

The court belongs to both players in the final analysis, and if one player leaves too much open space, his or her partner has an obligation to cover. For instance, if Smith runs around his forehand on return of serve, he naturally drifts into the backhand court. Lutz automatically moves over to cover the forehand side at net when this happens.

ball crosscourt with a firm but perhaps not excessively hard backhand—generally a safe crosscourt chip designed to force the server to make a low volley or half-volley coming in. Rather than thinking attack, the second-court player must be warier than his partner of the opposing net player's inclination to poach, particularly on first serves. And there is greater pressure inherent in the scoring situation itself. If his team is down love—15, he knows he must at least keep the ball in play or his team will go down love—30. These technical considerations create certain emotional nuances special to each position.

The first-court player becomes the natural aggressor on the team. He or she feels more intent on making the difficult shot, and more willing to go for the shot, win or lose. But, in taking greater risks, he puts his identity on the line more clearly. When the first-court player loses a point, it is usually fairly obvious. More appears to be riding on his actions, and so he reacts more extremely than his partner—he feels high when he helps to win a point, and more dejected when he loses it.

The second-court player is more conservative in his returns and in his reactions. He must be, in order to keep the ball in play. But when he fails to do that, it does not seem quite so important. If his partner lost the first point, he is only continuing the losing trend. If his partner won the first point, he is merely dropping them back into a tie. So the second-court player does not risk his ego so much, and becomes the steadier emotional force of the two.

The most sobering fact about the second-court player's position is that advantage points are always played in his court. His partner in the first court may have set up the ad with spectacular play, but he must seal the victory with solid, high-percentage tennis.

Now let's try to solve the problem of who should play which side in just the opposite way—by putting the strong forehand player in the backhand court.

In this arrangement, the first-court player concentrates on playing steady, striving to get the first point or the deuce point in order to put the pressure on the opponents. Meanwhile, the second court player is licensed to take a more explosive approach to receiving serve, which can add to the pressure. The second-court player concentrates on bringing his or her strong forehand into play by running around as many serves as possible, dipping his returns crosscourt, down the middle, or down the line, forcing low volleys or half-volleys. The player stands over in the alley in order to use the forehand fully, and remembers to recover toward the center of the court after each return. The extra footwork and other shot-preparation required is no problem because, if you are in fact stronger on the forehand side, you will be able to move to that position more quickly and confidently. Your only worry will be the ace served down the middle—a slight risk—or the kick serve into your body—a bigger threat depending on the server you face.

There are good examples of both types of teams which points up the real message about team composition: *Balance is everything*. Both players on a team must be capable of hitting offensive *or* defensive shots in given situations in a match, obviously. Yet when both players are constantly on the attack, or both are constantly playing a tentative or defensive game, their chances as a team are not as good. So one player must, over the long haul, be slightly more offensive both in his stroke-making and his attitude, in order for both players to present the greatest and most varied challenge to their opponents. Even this must be contradicted in part, in view of the effectiveness of such teams as Bob Hewitt and Frew McMillan, who are equally steady on their returns.

If there is a left-hander in the pair, that player would normally be in the second court regardless of who better fits the aggressor role. This in fact can make for a strong doubles team, with the supreme example in modern times being the much-titled combination of right-handed

John Newcombe and left-handed Tony Roche. Both have dependable first serves, move to net quickly, volley exceedingly well, and—with their common ground as fellow Aussies—have solid emotional ties to boot. In fact, of all the doubles teams of the past decade, the Newcombe-Roche team have consistently given us the most trouble.

When a team is balanced as we've suggested, the nonaggressor will tend to have a somewhat more detached attitude toward the play, and as a result a better perspective on the evolution of the match. This player therefore has the potential to lead the team, certainly not with the obvious and sustained play-making role of a football quarterback, say, but in a much more subtle way that in no manner reduces the possible value of such leadership. Slightly more removed from the heat of the action, and less vulnerable to emotional highs and lows, this player can keep tabs on how the strategy for the match is working out, and anchor the team psychologically.

Such captaincy, or team leadership, is in actual fact usually a floating role. For example, aside from who is playing which court, or whose mental approach is naturally more objective, there is the question of who happens to be on their game a bit more on the day of a match. Obviously, a player having technical problems, or low on confidence, or demoralized or distracted by other matters, is in no position to lead the team, and it then becomes the duty of the other player to assume that role, even if that player is also taking all the risks in the first court. One thing is for sure: If both players lack the confidence or flair or detachment to direct the match, the play of the team will become increasingly unfocused and disorganized.

In forming your own doubles partnerships—whether they be intended for the day or the season—you will always have to compromise a bit in your search for the well-balanced duo. But your team effectiveness will definitely improve if you consciously select partners who complement—*complement,* not duplicate—your own stroke-making skills, personality, and experience, and if you encourage those traits in your partner and yourself which help you mesh gears on court. For example, if you are playing with someone who is wiser in the ways of doubles, and you ask him questions that show you expect him or her to be in charge, you will generally find that that player will be more likely to lead the team effort so that both of you benefit.

Also, remember that circumstances in an actual match may force you to change your role from aggressor to captain and perhaps back again. You must be sufficiently flexible to note and accept the changes and to make the most of things in your given or chosen role. For example, if your normally mild-mannered partner becomes fired up all at once and starts hitting the all-out Superman shots you have been specializing in, don't try to ignore or discourage the development—especially if the shots are going in. Let your teammate fulfill the aggressive role while you pay more attention to the progress of your match from the vantage point of analyst and team captain.

It's also to your advantage to pick a doubles partner who balances you in other stroke-making departments besides the return of serve. Both of you must be able to serve consistently, but if one player tends to slice his serves and the other tends to twist or kick them, your partnership will be that much stronger for the variety of your joint attack.

Both of you must know how to volley and be willing to poach. But it is really not essential that both players have first-rate overheads, at least not in club play. As long as one of you can put away high balls with confidence, your team will be safe from the majority of lobs hit by your opponents. Similarly, if only one of you is of the speed-demon variety, that may provide enough of the court mobility your team requires at the club level of play.

CHAPTER 9

Moving As a Team

WE HAVE TALKED about the formation of a good doubles team according to our theory of balanced stroke-making abilities, supported by the appropriate emotional stance and leadership roles. Now let's examine how a team should function, once it is formed.

Good doubles partners reveal the quality of their teamwork in the manner in which they respond to each other's movements on the court, and to lobs and shots down the middle by the opponents. We've already suggested that moving as a team is one of the basic principles of modern doubles, and instrumental in insuring proper coverage of your team's side of the court. And we have outlined the mutually supportive roles of server and server's partner, and receiver and receiver's partner, in terms of aggressive doubles tactics.

But we haven't really looked at all the situations that spontaneously arise in doubles in which teamwork—who goes where and does what—is really tested. Your ability to move as a team can be measured quite accurately by how well you plug the holes put in your defenses by the opposing team's shots. By familiarizing yourself with these situations and learning the correct moves to make in each, it becomes only a matter of time and experience before you are instinctively moving and performing as a team.

Remember that such moves will come more readily if you understand that, even though you may not be involved in an exchange, you are *always* involved in the point. Sometimes players drift into stagnant moods if they haven't hit a ball for a while—they become spectators rather than participants. That's usually when the risk of a gap opening up on their side of the court is greatest.

RIDE WITH THE TIDE

Your principal doubles move is to get more or less side by side whether you're on the attack, or on the defense or in a defensive position. That's why you move into net whenever you can following serve or return—to join your partner and form a solid line of attack. That's also why you must retreat from net when your partner is forced back to the baseline. As soon as the partner tosses up a defensive lob, scoot back to the baseline.

When you and your partner are together at net or at the baseline, and one of you is pulled wide by an opponent's shot, the other should slide over a couple of steps in that direction, in order to close the gap between you. But don't move over so far that a gap is created on *your* side. Preserving the right space between you is a delicate balancing act, akin to keeping a rowboat afloat when one passenger leans out too far on one side.

COVER THE POACHER'S COURT

When you see your partner at net cross and poach on a shot, you should immediately shift into the half of the court your teammate has left vacant. If you have stayed back following your serve or return, this move should be relatively easy for you. If you have begun moving toward net, however, you will have to break stride in order to get into a position to protect your partner's newly vacated territory. It's vital, just in case the opponents get your partner's poach back.

Often in doubles it is a good idea to beat a partial retreat on your half of the court if your partner has moved extremely close to the net, say on a second volley following serve. With you already at net as the server's partner, your team is immediately highly vulnerable to a lob or lob-volley. By stepping back to the service line on your side, you put yourself into position to effectively field any lob, yet remain sufficiently forward to step in and volley a shot, or otherwise preserve your team's forward attacking posture.

NET PLAYER FIELDS MOST LOB RETURNS OF SERVE

If your serve is returned by way of a shallow lob over your partner's head, your partner should be in a position to sidestep back and put the ball away with an overhead smash. The net player really should be able to cover all lobs over his head unless he is poaching or playing extremely close to the net for some reason. If, however, the lob is deep, you as server may have to take responsibility for chasing it down, even if you have moved in a few steps in anticipation of volleying a return. Chances are you will have to lob back. In the meantime, your partner should have crossed and moved back to the service line.

In all uncertain situations created by the lob, remember to communicate your moves to your partner if he or she is not in a position to see them.

PLAYER MOVING TO NET TAKES BALL DOWN THE MIDDLE

Shots hit down the middle can severely test a team's ability to work together. As a rule, if one player is moving to net and the other player is already at net, the player in motion should take responsibility for any ball hit down the middle. So, if you're following a serve or a return into net, don't depend on your partner to volley away a shot hit between you. Because you are in motion, you should have a slight edge over your partner in anticipation and in stroking aggressively.

WITH BOTH PLAYERS AT NET, LAST PLAYER TO HIT TAKES BALL DOWN MIDDLE

If both players are already at net and a ball is hit between them, the player on the volleying side who last hit the ball should hit it again, because he or she will be marginally better prepared for making the shot. That said, we should immediately add that, if the other player feels he can make a stronger volley from that side than his partner, he should step in and take the ball.

USE FOREHAND TO SMASH SHALLOW LOB

If a shallow lob is hit to the middle, the player who can make the overhead with the forehand side should always make the shot. Few players, even among the pros, can smash decisively with their backhand. For that reason you should not hesitate to step well into your partner's side, if necessary, to relieve your partner of this awkward shot and to put the ball away with your forehand smash.

REPEAT THE PLAYS THAT WORK

If a sequence of actions by you and your partner seems to work well on a certain point or against a certain team, don't hesitate to repeat the sequence whenever you can. One such play that we have evolved in our years of doubles together has been extremely effective at times. In this play, Smith runs around and hits a forehand return of serve, then moves into the second court while Lutz, at net, crosses into the first court. The play confuses opponents and often forces weak shots. When it works, it's a great example of teamwork in motion.

CHAPTER 10

How to Help Your Partner Help You

A SUBSTANTIAL DEGREE of communication between partners —even when unspoken—greatly increases the effectiveness of any doubles team. Of all ideas related to doubles play, this idea of communication between partners is perhaps the most overpreached and underpracticed—or, at least, not practiced in any meaningful fashion—of all the ideas common in doubles debates. There are many superficial means of communication that don't help anyone, not just in tennis but in advertising and diplomacy, to name two other fields where, as everyone knows, there is often a lot of up-front communication but hardly any contact of substance.

Contact of substance between doubles partners must take place on the subject of strategy for the match, and at all critical high and low points during the match.

The first type of communication takes place, in part, even before

COMMUNICATE ON ALL CHANNELS

Good doubles partners get across to each other thoughts regarding tactics and technique, without becoming irritating or absurd in the process.

the match begins. You and your partner should be willing to talk openly about a strategic approach to playing your particular opponents, based on your strengths and their weaknesses, and come to some agreement on the subject before the match starts. In the next chapter we'll examine the variety of doubles teams one faces and the best tactics to use against each of them. For now, make sure you *both* "know the enemy," or at least that you both try to. If you've played among the same doubles teams for a long time, chances are you all know each other's weak points all too well. Even so, it doesn't hurt to remind your partner of the moment that Roger has an execrable overhead, or that Fifi is the type who gets more dangerous when her team falls behind. It is also a good idea to touch base with your partner beforehand about trying alternate formations, if it is at all likely that your opposition may force either possibility that day.

We've already discussed the key tactical decision of who should receive in which court. You must also decide who should serve first. Certainly, if the spin of the racket gives you the choice, your *team* should serve first. In singles it is sometimes advantageous to receive first, especially if you think you have a chance to break serve right off the bat. But if you give up the choice in doubles, the other team will certainly put their better server forward and thus in all likelihood start the match with a game in their pocket. So, whether you win the toss or not, make sure the more effective server on your side goes to the line first. And, in a really serious tournament match, make sure the stronger server serves first in each set, as the rules permit, *unless* the other player has been holding serve pretty well, in which case you should continue in the same order.

Bear in mind that the more effective server in doubles may not always be the *better* server of the two in singles. For instance a player who moves into net well following serve may be the more effective server in doubles even if the serve itself is nothing special.

Once a match is underway, keep your communication lines open in order to review and revise—and if necessary replace—your basic strategy according to the results you are getting and the level of play of the two teams.

There are plenty of chances for short chats between doubles partners—during every change of sides, for instance and, in club play, at frequent times in the course of collecting the balls for the server. Use these moments to propose changes in strategy, if your present strategy is failing, and to tip your partner off to your immediate plans. If your partner is serving and you mention that you are going to poach on the next point, the partner will concentrate on placing a serve that aids and abets your design. Or if you're receiving, and you tell your partner you are going to try a runaround forehand down the line, the other player will be on the lookout for a reflexed crosscourt volley from the opposing net player.

It is possible for the server's partner to use hand signals behind the back to inform the server of intentions to poach or not, before every serve. The trouble with a system of signals is that you have to keep using it to make it work—you can't just put your hand behind your back when you are going to poach, or the opponents will spot the signal right away—and that becomes tiresome. It can also become confusing if your partner misses or misunderstands the signal, and so defeats the whole purpose of the exercise.

Sometimes, in the heat of an exchange, there is time to shout instructions or information to one another that may well smooth your progress as a team. In some of the moves described in the preceding chapter, verbal tips to or from your partner could be exceedingly important.

There isn't usually time to call hard shots hit down the middle, but

((117))

calling shots helps in many other ambiguous spots. For instance, always call "Mine!" or "I've got it!" if you are in the process of going back for a lob that either of you could reach. Call "Back!" when you yourself throw up a lob from the backcourt, to prod your partner at net into an early start back to join you and so preserve your line of defense. And call "Cross!" when you are changing sides behind your partner and want to make sure he or she changes as well.

The other major form of verbal communication in doubles comes at critical high and low points during a match. Its purpose is to bolster a winning attitude, or to correct simple technical lapses in your partner's game.

A player's morale can drop sharply after hitting a poor shot on an important point in doubles. It is not simply the player's own conscience that erodes the morale—it is the player's sense of the real or imagined disapproval and disappointment of his or her partner. So, if you happen to be the partner in such a situation, your job is simply and cheerfully to utter something, or signal in some way, to get your partner's mind off that point and onto the next point. A long inspirational speech certainly isn't called for, but a few aptly chosen words may do the trick— if they sound sincere. If you can communicate that you still have faith in your partner's ability, and confidence in yourselves as a team, you may get both of you playing with renewed vigor. At the least, you'll minimize the psychological effects of your partner's lapse in play—on you and on your partner—and keep the opponents from suddenly running away with the match.

With some partners, a humorous remark may be the right approach. Raul Ramirez and Brian Gottfried, who comprise one of the top young doubles teams on the circuit today, sometimes laugh at each other's mistakes to relieve the tension and to get the slumping player relaxed and hitting all out again.

The worst thing you can do in a losing situation is to criticize or belittle your partner in word, thought, or deed. By word, we mean explicitly stating your criticism: "Alice, you always let us down on the big ones," or "Pat, that backhand of yours belongs in Mme Tussaud's Chamber of Horrors."

By deed, we mean frowning, scowling, or sighing audibly, after your partner has double-faulted or otherwise erred in your eyes.

And by thought, we mean the simple abandonment of confidence in your partner. You may think you are keeping your pessimistic view to yourself, but your partner will sense it almost immediately, and then you are finished as a team.

Admittedly it is sometimes hard to avoid giving up on a partner if the other player's showing has been particularly dismal. On the other hand, never underestimate the power of a stubborn optimism in turning a match around. It may take extraordinary patience on your part, and a few more games of struggling, but if your attitude is sincere it just might break through and inspire your partner at last and, with a lucky shot here and there, combine to give you the winning momentum. Exactly such shifts have occurred so many times in doubles matches among the pros that we assume they occur with equal frequency in the amateur game.

Doubles partners should also be sure to communicate when they find themselves well *ahead* in a match. The danger of losing the momentum in doubles is so real that you should always be on the lookout for complacency on your side. If you sense that your partner is being lulled into a lower standard of play, urge him or her to "help me break their serve one more time," or "let's bear down on them these last few games"—anything to get the partner playing more aggressively again. Complacency and an unrealistically favorable view of the match will show up in an increased number of attempts at low-percentage shots, or in a generally lackadaisical attitude toward such things as getting first serves in, or returning well.

If you have established an open and effective playing relationship with your doubles partner, you should be able to exchange brief technical or strategic tips in the course of a match without injured feelings on either side. Such freedom and flexibility represents the highest level of mutual tolerance and understanding in doubles play. It also adds to your effectiveness as a team. In effect, the arrangement equips your team with a self-regulating device for keeping your tennis game in tune under pressure.

Some players simply will not accept advice from their partners and, indeed, may find that instructional prattle of any kind tends to destroy their concentration. Other players may react adversely if the advice is delivered with too much authority, or if it appears to be rather simple-minded for their level of play. For example, telling a partner who is having trouble with the serve to "Get your first serve in," may merely rub salt in the wound without conveying any perception about the real problem. The oft-used bit of advice, "Keep your eye on the ball," is another phrase of doubtful value in a match. "What the hell do you think I'm doing?" a thin-skinned partner may reply. A moment's indiscretion on one player's part could leave the partnership in shambles.

Between partners who can take and receive honest and constructive criticism, however, there is much that can be communicated, provided it is kept short and specific.

If your partner is having trouble serving, it may be hard for you to offer practical advice on the stroke itself, for you are standing at the ready at net and not actually observing the service motion. But you may be able to deduce a technical flaw from where the ball is landing. If the serve consistently finishes in the net, your partner is probably tossing the ball too low; if it is landing too long, he or she may be tossing too high. In bouncing a ball back before the next serve, suggest, "Just toss a bit higher." Or your partner may be directing the serve into the receiver's strong side without realizing it, in which case a mere word from you can get the server to alter the placement intelligently.

You can observe your partner's service return more easily than the serve. If the player is returning with too open a stance, or standing flat-footed, or falling back from the serve, you might suggest, "Turn on the ball," or "Move into it."

On volleys you may notice that your partner is hitting too tentatively, without getting his or her body into the stroke. Suggest, "Meet the ball earlier."

If your partner is lobbing short, simply say, "Hit the baseline next time." When your partner misses an overhead, you can be sure your opponents will reserve their next high lob for the same player, so it is well worth your time to try to bolster your partner's confidence by saying, for instance, "Keep your head up a bit longer, that's all." If you give the player one positive thought to focus on for the next overhead, it may prevent a repeat of the mistake.

CAUTION: don't turn your doubles match into a playing lesson for your partner, whose personality simply may not tolerate your various perceptions about his or her game. Our suggestions here are merely intended as a sample of the kind of approach that can work with certain players, provided the observation is on target and the tone is right.

The one form of communication we don't recommend between doubles partners is a lot of apologizing. If you have a good team relationship, your partner knows you feel bad for having missed an easy poach, or for setting up the opponent for a winning smash. Your partner assumes you did not make the mistake on purpose, and therefore do not require forgiveness.

Tennis is a game of mistakes, and if you apologize for all your mis-hits, then the chorus of "I'm sorrys" will eventually get to your partner. Pretty soon he or she will be sorry, too—sorry you're out there on the team. If you constantly call attention to your fallibility as a player, imagined or real, it will genuinely increase your fallibility in the eyes of your partner. So, for your own sake and that of your team, remember that good doubles is never having to say you're sorry.

CHAPTER 11

How to Outplay Other Doubles Teams

IF SINGLES IS a battle of individual wills, then doubles is a battle of wits—with one collective strategy pitted against another and the smarter of the two usually coming out on top.

The ability to analyze an opposing team's strengths and weaknesses, and to exploit this information during play, is at least as important to success in doubles as in executing the basic doubles strokes, or playing with good doubles teamwork.

The best way to find out about the other team is to make mental notes on how they perform as you play, then later consciously to take stock of their assets and liabilities as a team.

Watch for individual soft spots or preferences in their groundstrokes, volleys, lobs, and overheads. Analyze the server's No. 1 and No. 2 serves. Note where the net player stands in relation to the net and the alley. Note the style of return of serve each player favors. Observe how the two players move as a team, how well they cover for each other, and how and when they communicate. Determine whether they're better baseliners or net players—few players are equally good in both parts of the court.

You can also learn much by watching a team play in another match, provided you study the course of the play with some concentration— it's easy to drift into a lazy spectator's role when you're on the sidelines and thereby gain no usable intelligence.

You can also inform yourself about an opposing team, at least to a certain extent, in the course of your prematch warmup and during the early part of your match. Even if it's your first encounter with them, you may be able to spot something that you can put to use right away.

DIVIDE AND CONQUER

This time-honored approach to all sort of things works in doubles, too.

A team with little experience of playing together will be vulnerable to divisive tactics. Against such a pairing, always hit more shots down the middle whenever you have the choice. Confusion on their part on taking volleys or fielding lobs can quickly lead to a loss of a sense of purpose as a team. They may even begin to argue, especially if winners are scored through the middle more than once or twice, and at the least feel disgruntled about their effectiveness as a team.

It is also good strategy to try to divide and conquer any time when there is a wide disparity of playing talent between your opponents. The fact is that doubles teams are seldom perfectly balanced in terms of the ability and experience of the individual players. In these cases, make the weaker player the target of your team's more aggressive shots. As you run off points with increasing regularity against the weaker player, his or her partner will become more and more frustrated. To make matters hotter, attack the weaker player until the player yields an easy high ball for your side, then drill that one past the better player, who will look and feel quite foolish as a result.

Don't confuse such tactics with gamesmanship. Taking advantage of a weaker opposing player is a legitimate doubles attack. If it reduces the camaraderie on the other side of the net, that will make your task even easier, but the blame for their decline in teamwork lies squarely on the other side. All you have done is play the smart shots.

A version of this attack also comes in handy when a usually strong opponent is having an off-day. The player may be having trouble with a particular stroke, or playing below par generally. Don't let the player keep the ball in play just on the basis of his or her reputation. Attack the player as you would the weakling, and his or her partner will begin to lose confidence in their chances in the match.

PLAY AGAINST THEM, NOT WITH THEM

There's a tendency among less experienced and perhaps less competitive doubles players to get into a pattern of play that suits the opposing team rather than its own.

Against a net player you know to be a confirmed poacher, don't float crosscourt returns, no matter how good your backhand feels that day. Hit down-the-line with the backhand or a runaround forehand to put the poacher on notice—and do it early in the match before the net player scores and builds up confidence.

Against a scrambling, hustling team with a fairly good net game, for example, it is suicidal to embark on extended rallies for the pure joy of rallying. Against such teams, you must go for percentage winners time and again, never permitting the ball to stay in play any longer than necessary. You have to try to overpower them—and to do it right from the start.

Against a power team with big serves and overheads and an aggressive net game, you have to try to play with more consistency. If you get caught up in a campaign to outgun them, you may find that you're making all the mistakes. Try to break the speed-and-power team's pace of play by keeping the ball low and hitting a lot of lobs and dinks. Keep taking the speed off their shots rather than trying to add some of your own. Bear down on returning serve—try to return as early as you can, and aim for the onrushing server's feet. Extend the play to every part of their side of the court and force a lot of overheads to tire them out and perhaps provoke that one overhead into the net that will unnerve them.

Against a team that likes to play from the baseline, try drop-volleys and angle all your volleys more sharply to the sidelines. Don't get into long exchanges of ground strokes with steady baseliners—unless you're steadier than they are.

This policy of playing your own game extends to individual shots. Don't be so impressed by one of your opponent's skill at down-the-line returns, say, or drop-volleys, that you start trying to emulate that player. Stick to the shots you know how to execute in order to keep your play steady and your confidence on the rise.

AVOID THEIR STRENGTHS

Challenging opponents in the strokes they play best is poor strategy, except as change of pace. Don't become so obsessed with a player's skill at one stroke that you start feeding balls to that stroke.

If you're playing an opponent who hits with extreme topspin, you may not be able to avoid dealing with it. Simply be prepared to defend against his or her shots with an eagle eye. A ball with heavy topspin dips through the air. It's especially easy to mis-hit on volleys or overheads because the timing must be precise. If you don't meet the ball in the center of your racket strings, it will fly up on you.

In serving, make sure you get the vast majority of balls to the receiver's backhand, if that is the weaker side. It is easier to attack the backhand from the first court if you can learn to hit some degree of kick or twist serve. You'll have to practice tossing the ball more over your head, and serving with your shoulders sidewise to the net for a longer interval, in order to start hitting up and over the ball and putting the kick spin on it.

In serving to the second court, it is easier to hit into the backhand corner if you stand more toward the sideline. The closer you get to the sideline, the more you open up the middle of the court to attack on the return. But if it is the opponent's forehand that is so worrisome, then this slight change in your position at the baseline won't hurt you at all.

If you can succeed in consistently avoiding serving to the side that your opponent excels in, you will be able to build up a pattern of coming in to volley. And the opponent will become frustrated and dispirited for not being able to hit from the favored side.

Against a first-rate receiver, you will not only have to vary the types of serves you hit and the position to which you hit them, but you must begin to vary your pattern of following serve as well. Stay back from time to time, to force the opponent to focus on a different aiming-point on the return. Mixing up what you do after serve may keep the receiver from getting grooved on the return.

In returning serve, don't resort to the lob against teams with exceptionally good overheads, except in an emergency. And don't attack the net player with too many hard returns if that player is a strong volleyer.

You may be able to confuse a good server from time to time by varying the normal depth at which you stand to receive. Stand a yard more behind the baseline and the opponent's perspective may be affected to the point where he or she serves long. Stand well in and you may elicit a serve into the net.

An opponent with an extreme slice serve can be especially effective against you in the first court, for the serve wide to your forehand will pull you off the court. If the extreme slice serve is your opponent's stock in trade, receive the ball a step closer to the sideline in the first court, so that you can move diagonally to hit it early on the bounce. If you wait for the ball to bounce to waist level, you'll be off the court.

A serve with extreme kick—an American twist—should never take you by surprise, because you can read it in the ball toss prior to the serve. If the opponent lifts the ball to the extreme over-the-head toss position, be ready for the ball to bounce to your left a bit more than usual. If you are not ready for it, the ball's quirky bounce may surprise you and force a mis-hit or weak return. The key is to move your feet the moment you see where the ball will bounce—to the extent that you may feel you are moving as you hit the ball.

You'll encounter the extreme twist serve more in the second court, since the ball bounces towards the sideline and can drag you off the court. It will be used in the first court more as a change-of-pace serve, and it can give you trouble there, too, since the ball tends to bounce up into your racket.

CHANGE YOUR FORMATION

There are two offbeat doubles formations, one for serving and the other for receiving, that are easy to learn and, when used in the correct tactical situation, highly effective. Pros resort to these formations all the time, but club players shy away from using them, or bring them into play at the wrong time. Yet club players could swiftly neutralize certain strengths of opposing teams if they would try these formations.

The odd serving formation is variously called the Australian or I-formation. We prefer the latter name because that precisely describes the alignment of the two players. Both you and your partner stand on the same side of the center and close to it, with you preparing to serve and your partner at net facing diagonally towards the receiver. This formation is worth trying against any receiver who has become so well grooved in making crosscourt returns of serve that he or she is hitting offensive shots or even winners off the serve. The changed formation forces the player to hit down the line instead of crosscourt—the net player is blocking the crosscourt path. The server moves into the open court following serve to handle the return.

The I-formation also can be effective against a receiver who almost always lobs the net player on return. The altered formation forces the receiver to lob crosscourt instead of down the line in the usual pattern. If the player sticks to lobbing down the line, the server is in good position to handle the shot.

The odd receiving formation simply positions both players at the baseline against a strong first serve. It is well worth trying if you face a strong serve-and-volley player who has been hitting winners off first or second volleys with consistency, or whose partner has been able to cross

In the I-formation, both players on the serving team line up on the same side of the court. The idea is to force a particularly strong receiver to break pattern and return down the line instead of crosscourt.

and poach on your weak returns with impunity.

By standing at the baseline, you force the opponents to volley at different depths and angles for their winners, thus changing their grooved pattern and perhaps forcing errors. Should they keep the ball in play, you must hit hard ground strokes, again to try to force volleying errors, and make lobs, looking to move up to net behind your first effectively deep lob.

HAMMER AWAY AT WEAKNESSES

By avoiding an opposing team's strengths, you will probably be automatically exploiting their weaknesses, but there are several specific plays worth emphasizing.

For instance, the patsy second serve is one of the most vulnerable shots in tennis, yet countless players at the club level manage to get away with it, because their opponents handle it improperly.

Nothing is more frustrating to a receiving team than for one of its members to drill an easy setup either into the net or off into the bleachers somewhere. It's like throwing money away.

One reason many easy returns are missed is the receiver's failure to move in at least a couple of steps for the second serve. If you know the serve is going to be short, give yourself a head start on playing it correctly and be in position to move into the shot smartly. Haste makes wasted effort. When the ball does float in, move in and hit it before it has begun to sag downward.

Another reason club players have trouble with the patsy second serve is that the ball comes in so slowly they forget to move their feet even if they have moved into proper position following the first serve. The slower the shot, the more you have to consciously shift your weight

((131))

Many doubles players fail to hammer away at the weaknesses that crop up in opposing teams. One of the most conspicuous soft spots in doubles is the weak serve, against which any self-respecting doubles team must move with ferocity and zeal. A good way to keep your energies in check when you "run around" a soft serve to your backhand is simply to target on the service line in the opposing court.

into it, and to do that you must move your feet.

Finally, always pick a spot to hit with your return of a duck second serve. Many players, realizing that they have an obvious setup, simply bash the ball as hard as they can and think that will do the job. The ball usually sails out. A good aiming-point is the service line or a few feet past the service line. Aiming well within the court in this manner will keep you from overhitting and still permit you to play the return aggressively. Even if the return bounces way inside the baseline, it will have such pace that it will keep the opponent on the defensive.

If there is a particularly weak server on the opposing team, make sure you and your partner put the heat on that player when receiving. Move in to net behind *all* your returns. Breaking that service may hold the key to your winning the match, so bear down. And don't forget to nail the server's partner at net with some of your returns, if you can, to add insult to injury and destroy their team morale.

Keep track of your own serving performance and observe what types of serve appear to give opponents the most trouble. Don't stick with your preconceived notions on serving if results in the match bear out different conclusions. For example, some players return better against fast serves than slower, sliced, or kick serves. So, although you may feel you are serving well because the ball is going in and at a good rate of speed, if it's coming back effectively, that good feeling of yours isn't going to help the team effort much. Therefore, switch to hitting with more spin—you may win a string of points before your opponent has adjusted his or her footwork to the new serve.

Above all, when serving in doubles, *never double-fault against the weaker receiver on the other team.* Any time a player misses an easy overhead, you have that player on the ropes emotionally, and you and your partner must give the player a chance to blow still another overhead as soon as you can. Remember, the overhead more than any other stroke in tennis, is a confidence shot—and without confidence it's an easy shot to miss three or four times running.

Height, or lack of it, is sometimes a weakness you can exploit in tennis. Big players may be harder to pass with lobs, but their reflexes are usually a bit slower and they are therefore more vulnerable to shots hit right at them at net. Smaller players are usually quicker and cover the court better, but they often can be attacked with balls that bounce high, particularly to their backhand side.

Sometimes a weakness may be built into the way a doubles team assumes its various formations in the course of a game. Any time opponents deviate from their normal positions, in serving, receiving, or playing at net, a bell should go off in your head to alert you to a possible lapse in thinking or a change in strategy on their part, and to your means for adapting to or exploiting that change.

If the opponent stands a step wider to serve, you move a step wider to receive. If the net player has moved in close to net, consider lobbing on the return. If the player has stepped farther back, shelve the lob alternative for the time being on the return. If the player has inched more toward center, think of hitting a passing shot down the line—unless you feel that that is what the net player is trying to get you to think.

VARIATIONS FOR PLAYING LEFTIES

There seem to be a disproportionate number of left-handers playing tennis, so make sure you know the special challenge of playing lefties and then get some direct experience of hitting with them so that lefties can't use their novelty to confuse and exploit you.

The keys to playing lefties in doubles are straightforward.

When serving to a left-hander, you must reverse your usual target areas, in order to attack the player's backhand. In other words, in the first court you must direct the majority of your serves wide, and not down the center as you would attempt to do against a right-hander. And in the second court—which is where lefties will usually play doubles, to avail themselves of more forehands—you must serve down the center rather than wide.

When receiving serve, you must be ready for the ball to slice or spin in the opposite direction from what you would expect on a right-hander's serve. A leftie's slice serve to the second court is especially effective, because it pulls the receiver off the court. So, when returning a left-handed serve in that court, stand a step closer to the sideline and be prepared to quickly recover into your court after making the return.

In both courts, be prepared to hit backhands that are somewhat farther from your body then usual. And until you're quite used to the left-hander's particular serve, don't attempt to move into net following your return.

When the left-hander is at net in doubles, do your best to avoid his or her forehand volley, which is likely to produce very sharply angled shots. Hit down the middle of the court and you will be hitting into the backhands of both players, with the exception of the one situation in which the leftie occupies the first court, for serving. When the leftie's partner is serving in the second court, the leftie is vulnerable to the passing shot or lob down the line.

KEEP YOUR GAME PLAN TO YOURSELVES

For every offense there is a good defense in tennis, and that's why, no matter how many shots and tactics you and your partner are able to develop, there will always be a team that can fight back—especially if they know what they are fighting. So never deliberately reveal your game plan to opponents. Often at the club level friendly opponents will exchange remarks like, "I'm going to test your overhead today," or "Watch out on your backhand side." Such remarks actually prepare players for hitting their weak shots with greater concentration—and often more success. So don't talk strokes or strategy to opponents under any circumstances.

In actual play, you will necessarily put into action your analysis of the opposing team's strengths and weaknesses. But by playing the occasional change-of-pace shot, especially on serve and return of serve, you can obscure your main attack/defense plan to a far greater extent than you might expect. And you would be surprised at how many teams will be befuddled by a seemingly obvious ploy like standing to serve in the I-formation.

Stick to your game plan, but sprinkle it with random moves and shots from time to time, and don't hesitate to invent and improvise, especially on noncrucial points. Behind such a smokescreen you will be patiently carving out your victory.

CHAPTER 12

Getting the Winning Edge

ONCE YOU UNDERSTAND the basic shots and ploys in doubles, and have had the experience of playing with a variety of partners against a variety of teams, so that you are reasonably competent in the game and reasonably familiar with some of the things that can go wrong —and others that can go right—you will probably become a doubles fanatic. The preliminary stages of learning doubles are often fraught with tension and frustration, but in time the doors will open to the rich and varying challenge that the game really is. By then you won't be able to get enough of it.

To continue to make progress in the game after this point—that is, to win more matches than your natural level of play entitles you to— you will have to learn to compete more shrewdly and intensely. Without attempting to go into the mysteries of competitiveness, we would like to point out the main techniques and approaches to physical and mental fitness that we think can make all sorts of players more effective competitors in doubles.

((137))

POSTMORTEMS ON MATCHES

Never let any doubles match fade in your memory until you have at least reflected somewhat on the composition of the two teams, the key shots and tactics during the match, and the reasons one team won and the other team lost. Force yourself to draw at least one conclusion from the events of the match.

This postmortem process can be as simple as noting that you weren't getting enough of your first serves in, or one of your opponents should have been attacked more on the overhead, or your side upheld the principles of moving as a team better than the other side. You might even write down your conclusions in a notebook after every match, at least until this pattern of conscious observation is an established habit. In this manner, you will gradually build up a catalog of information about yourself, the types of opponents, and the nature of doubles itself that will prove invaluable in future matches.

Seeing one's tennis strokes on videotape has proven to be an effective instructional technique. You can also profit by "instant replays" of your doubles matches, in the various forms we've suggested.

Involve your partner, or even your opponents, in a chat about the match afterward, if you can. Other views often shed light on matters you were ignoring or misunderstanding. If you can get your local tennis professional, or some other knowledgeable player, to give you a critique of a match he or she has watched, lend an attentive ear.

PRACTICE

Practice builds consistency in your stroke-making and helps to eliminate any soft spots in your game.

It brings your overall play up to a level that is more solid and reliable. Natural ability may carry you through any number of matches. But, unless you studiously work on all your strokes and shots, you may find that your tennis career is dotted with spectacular highs and lows. One day you may hit everything absolutely perfectly. Another day you are at rock-bottom. And when you get killed by someone, even if it is someone you have consistently beaten before, it shakes your confidence.

Only practice can develop your game so that it has fewer peaks and valleys—and so that your confidence isn't always on a yo-yo as a result.

You can practice doubles skills alone to a degree, though for most players this is a boring, monkish enterprise. Yet there is much to be said for working on your serve solitarily, provided you give your entire concentration to the matter, and keep the sessions short. Focus on the toss, on staying fluid, and on hitting to specific targets.

You can work a bit on your volley by hitting against a wall. Stand far enough away so that you are simulating the range you would need for a first volley, and strive to meet the ball in front of yourself.

Your volley stroke will also firm up if you work on strengthening your wrists by squeezing a ball, or some similar exercise device, in the age-old manner of determined tennis jocks.

A short session with another player—ideally your regular doubles partner—makes for a far more enjoyable workout. Play to the doubles lines on the court and alternate practicing serves and service returns

((139))

as though there were opponents positioned at net. Be sure to switch courts—and also to switch sides, if you're playing outdoors, to take full advantage of the range of natural wind and sun conditions from both sides.

You can both practice lobs and overheads at the same time. In fact, this work may yield higher dividends than any other form of practice, since you probably give less attention to these strokes than any other. And two players can develop each other's lobs and overheads quite naturally in practice.

Finally, you can practice volleying. Stand in opposing service boxes and concentrate on keeping the ball in play rather than going for winners. That will build your racket control and your ability to go from one side to the other. You can play games on the basis of this "mini-tennis" drill, serving underhanded and working on your volleys and half-volleys, developing your touch and tuning up your reflexes at the net.

A half-hour practice session devoted in ten-minute segments to serve-return, lob-overhead, and volleys, is great way for you and your regular partner to brush up on doubles shot-making.

PHYSICAL CONDITIONING

The doubles game that we have tried to communicate in this book attempts to bring out power and speed to the best of your ability for the level of play you enjoy. It is not as rigorous an exercise as singles but, as we have suggested you play it, the game still demands a certain level of physical readiness, speed of reflex, and good muscle tone. So it comes down to a question of how much you are prepared to build yourself up to play the best doubles you can.

For most players, a game of tennis two or three times a week comprises their entire fitness program. They do not have the time or the inclination to do anything else to raise the level of their general fitness.

Additional work will sharpen your doubles play if you have the gumption and desire for it. And certainly it will improve your general well-being. It is particularly worth considering if your energy level—and thus quality of play—drops sharply in the doubles matches you are playing at present. When you are tired, serving becomes a chore and three overheads in a row nearly benches you. You begin to stand flat-footed on returns and to hit off your back foot. You "hope" lobs out rather than scampering back to field them. You need to get in better shape.

Running or jogging builds up your legs and stretches your endurance but, like solo practice sessions, it's too boring for many players to keep up on any regular basis.

A more interesting approach might be a combination of skipping rope and running wind sprints. A program of skipping rope, which can be done anywhere, builds up the legs and arms, and has the additional merit for tennis of making you quicker on your feet. Running wind sprints, in moderation, prepares you for the short bursts of speed that tennis doubles demands, in coming to net following your serve, in rushing in after aggressive returns, or for other emergencies occasioned by some opponent's skillful lob or drop shot. Quick bursts of speed take a lot of energy and casual jogging will not equip you for them.

Exercises to build your stomach muscles can make you surprisingly more solid in your stroke-making. The stomach is the center of your body and in certain ways really controls your entire body. All your movements on the tennis court are either initiated or controlled by the stomach. If your stomach isn't firm, you will not be able to stretch effectively for your serve, and you won't move from side to the side with as

Doubles is not for the lazy or indifferent. If you want to play to the best of your ability, you really must first get your body in shape for the necessary exertions. Smith recommends jogging, wind sprints, rope-skipping, and leg lifts (for the stomach) for maximizing your doubles potential.

much authority. Finally, you won't hit through your shots as firmly. Sit-ups and leg lifts in a variety of forms are ideal for building up the stomach muscles.

A final benefit of a stronger stomach by the way, is a stronger back. Most people who lead sit-down lives—for work or pleasure—gradually lose strength and elasticity in their lower back muscles. The older you get, the more a weak lower back can inhibit your movements and spoil your fun. Keep your stomach muscles in good shape and they'll be able to do some of the work involved in bending, running, and swinging, and so you'll put less strain on your back muscles.

PREMATCH PREPARATION

Most club players warm up for a match with just their hitting arm. The rest of the body stays cold and tight. As a result, they may not really play with properly loosened muscles until well into the match. That means they're not stroking or moving to the best of their ability.

Limbering up before a match is also a relatively slight investment in time for the protection against strains and other injuries that it provides. Here's a routine of stretching exercises that can be accomplished in 10 minutes—surely not too much time for even the busiest executive. You'll feel greased and oiled and ready to go after you've done them. Jog around the court three times, then perform as follows (and as illustrated on next pages):

1. Rotate head 360° to limber up the neck muscles. Both ways, a half-dozen times each way.

2. Rotate shoulder muscles for a minute.

3. Rotate hips for a minute.

4. Swing arms around in windmill fashion until hands tingle.

((*143*))

Whether you're playing doubles on an occasional or a regular basis, make sure you devote 10 to 15 minutes to stretching your muscles before every match, to get them properly oiled and to avoid possible strains and sprains. Lutz keeps things loose by following a simple stretching regimen before every match or workout.